ALSO BY JAN CHOZEN BAYS

How to Train a Wild Elephant: And Other Adventures in Mindfulness

Jizo Bodhisattva: Guardian of Children, Travelers, and Other Voyagers

Mindful Eating: A Guide to Rediscovering a Healthy and Joyful Relationship with Food

The Vow-Powered Life: A Simple Method for Living with Purpose

Mindfulness on the Go

Simple Meditation Practices
You Can Do Anywhere

Jan Chozen Bays, MD

SHAMBHALA
Boulder
2014

Shambhala Publications, Inc.
4720 Walnut Street
Boulder, Colorado 80301
www.shambhala.com

This book is an abridged edition of
How to Train a Wild Elephant (Shambhala, 2011).

14 13 12 11 10 9 8 7

Printed in Canada

♾This edition is printed on acid-free paper that meets the American National Standards Institute z39.48 Standard.
♻Shambhala Publications makes every effort to print on recycled paper. For more information please visit www.shambhala.com.
Distributed in the United States by Penguin Random House LLC and in Canada by Random House of Canada Ltd

See page 233 for Library of Congress Cataloging-in-Publication data.

Contents

Mindfulness on the Go

Introduction

People often say to me, "I'd love to practice mindfulness, but I'm so busy I can't seem to find the time."

Most people think of mindfulness as something they must squeeze into an already full schedule of working, raising children, caring for a home. In truth, making mindfulness part of your life is more like a game of connect the dots, or like a paint-by-numbers kit. Do you remember those pictures where each small area is labeled with a number that tells you which color to use? As you fill in all the brown areas, then the greens and the blues, a pleasing picture begins to emerge.

Mindfulness practice is like that. You

begin with one small area of your life, let's say how you answer the phone. Each time the phone rings, you pause to take three long, slow breaths before you pick it up. You do this for a week or so, until it becomes a habit. Then you add another mindfulness practice, such as mindful eating. Once this way of being present is integrated into your life, you add another. Gradually you are present and aware for more and more moments of the day. The pleasing experience of an awakened life begins to emerge.

The exercises in this book point to many different spaces in your life that you can begin to fill in with the warm colors of openhearted mindfulness. I am a meditation teacher, and I live at a Zen monastery in Oregon. I'm also a pediatrician, a wife, a mother, and a grandmother, so I understand well how stressful and challenging daily life can become. I developed many of these exercises to help me be more aware, happy, and at ease within the flow of a busy life. I offer this collection to anyone who would like to become more fully present and enjoy the small moments of their life. You don't have to go to a month-long meditation retreat or move to a monastery to restore peace and balance to your life. They are already available to you. Bit by bit, daily mindfulness practice will help you uncover satisfaction and fulfillment in the very life you are living now.

What Is Mindfulness and Why Is It Important?

In recent years, interest in mindfulness has grown enormously among researchers, psychologists, physicians, educators, and among the general public. There's now a significant body of scientific research indicating the benefits of mindfulness for mental and physical health. But what exactly do we mean by "mindfulness"?

Here's the definition I like to use:

> Mindfulness is deliberately paying full attention to what is happening around you and within you—in your body, heart, and mind. Mindfulness is awareness without criticism or judgment.

Sometimes we are mindful, and sometimes we are not. A good example is paying attention to your hands on the steering wheel of a car. Remember when you were first learning to drive, and how the car wobbled and wove its way along the road as your hands clumsily jerked the wheel back and forth, correcting and overcorrecting? You were wide awake, completely focused on the mechanics of driving. After a while your hands learned to steer well, making subtle and automatic adjustments. You could keep the car moving smoothly ahead without paying any conscious attention to your hands. You could drive, talk, eat, and listen to the radio, all at the same time.

Thus arises the experience we have all had, of driving on automatic pilot. You open the car door, search for your keys, back carefully out of the driveway, and . . . you pull into the parking garage at work. Wait a minute! What happened to twenty miles and forty minutes between house and job? Were the lights red or green? Your mind took a vacation, in some pleasant or distressing realm, as your body deftly maneuvered your car through flowing traffic and stoplights, suddenly awakening as you arrived at your destination.

Is that bad? It's not bad in the sense of something you should feel ashamed or guilty about. If you are able to drive to work on autopilot for years without having an accident, that's pretty skillful! We could say that it's sad, though, because when we spend a lot of time with our body doing one thing while our mind is on vacation somewhere else, it means that we aren't really present for much of our life. When we aren't present, it makes us feel vaguely but persistently dissatisfied. This sense of dissatisfaction, of a gap between us and everything and everyone else, is the essential problem of human life. It leads to those moments when we are pierced with a feeling of deep doubt and loneliness.

The Buddha called it the First Truth: the fact that every person will at some time experience this kind of distress. There are many happy moments in our lives, of course, but when our friends go home, when we are lonely or tired, when we feel disappointed or sad or betrayed, then dissatisfaction and unhappiness emerge once again.

We all try over-the-counter remedies—food, drugs, sex, overwork, alcohol, movies, shopping, gambling—to relieve the pain of ordinary life as a human being. All of these remedies work for a little while, but most of them have side effects—such as being in debt, blacking out, getting arrested, or losing someone we love—so they only increase our distress in the long run.

The labels on over-the-counter remedies say, "For temporary relief of symptoms only. If symptoms persist, see your doctor." Over the course of many years I have found one reliable remedy for the relief of recurrent discomfort and unhappiness. I have prescribed it for myself and for many other people, with excellent results. It is regular mindfulness practice.

Much of our dissatisfaction with life will disappear, and many simple joys will emerge, if we can learn to be present with things just as they are.

You've already experienced moments of mindful awareness. Everyone can recall at least one time when they were completely awake, when everything became clear and vivid. We call these peak moments. They can happen when we experience something unusually beautiful or poignant, such as the birth of a child or the passing of a loved one. It can also happen when our car goes into a skid. Time slows down as we watch the accident unfold or not. But it doesn't have to be dramatic. It can happen on an ordinary walk, as we turn a corner and everything is, for a moment, luminous.

What we call peak moments are times when we are completely aware. Our life and our awareness are undivided, at one. At these times the gap between us and everything else closes and suffering disappears. We feel satisfied. Actually we are beyond satisfaction and dissatisfaction. We are present. We are Presence. We get a tantalizing taste of what Buddhists call the enlightened life.

These moments inevitably fade, and there we are again, separate and grumpy about it. We can't force peak moments or enlightenment to happen. The tools of mindfulness, however, can help us close the gaps that cause our unhappiness. Mindfulness unifies our body, heart, and mind, bringing them together in focused attention. When we are thus unified, the barrier between "me" and "everything else" becomes thinner and thinner until, in a moment, it vanishes! For a while, often a brief moment or occasionally a lifetime, all is whole, all is holy, all is at peace.

The Benefits of Mindfulness

There are many benefits of mindfulness practice. Research on happiness conducted by Kirk Warren Brown and Richard M. Ryan at the University of Rochester shows that "people high in mindfulness are models of flourishing and positive mental health." It is good for all ailments of your heart and mind, and even of your body. But don't believe me just because I said so. Try the exercises in this book for a year and discover how they change your own life.

Here are a few of the benefits of mindfulness that I have found.

1. Mindfulness conserves energy

It is fortunate that we can learn to do tasks skillfully. It is unfortunate that this skill enables us to go unconscious as we do them. It is unfortunate because when we go unconscious, we are missing out on large parts of our life. When we "check out," our mind tends to go to one of three places: the past, the future, or the fantasy realm. These three places have no reality outside our imagination. Right here where we are is the only place, and right now the only time, we are actually alive.

The capacity of the human mind to recall the past is a unique gift. It helps us learn from our errors and change an unhealthy life direction. However, when the mind doubles back to the past, it often begins to ruminate endlessly on our past mistakes. "If only I'd said this . . . , then she would have said that . . ." Unfortunately the mind seems to think we are very stupid. It calls up the errors of our past over and over, blaming and criticizing us repeatedly. We wouldn't pay to rent and watch the same painful movie 250 times, but somehow we let our mind replay a bad memory over and over, each time experiencing the same distress and shame. We wouldn't remind a child 250 times of a small mistake he or she made, but somehow we allow our mind to continue to call up the past and to inflict anger and shame upon our own inner small being. It seems that our mind is afraid that we will fall prey to bad judgment, ignorance, or inattention yet again. It doesn't believe that actually we are smart—smart enough to learn from one mistake, and not to repeat it.

Ironically, a mind filled with anxiety is likely to create what it most fears. The anxious mind doesn't realize that when it pulls us into daydreams of regret about the past, we are not attending to the present. When we are unable to be present, we tend not to act wisely or skillfully. We are more likely to do the very thing the mind worries we will do.

The capacity of the human mind to plan for the future is another of our unique gifts. It gives us a road map and compass to steer by. It decreases the chances that we will make a wrong turn and end up caught in a long detour. It increases the chances that we will arrive at the end of life satisfied with our life path and what we have accomplished.

Unfortunately the mind, in its anxiety for us, tries to make plans for a huge number of possible futures, most of which will never arrive. This constant leapfrogging into the future is a waste of our mental and emotional energy. The most important way we can prepare for the unknown-to-come is to make a reasonable plan and then to pay attention to what is happening right now. Then we can greet what flows toward us with a clear, flexible mind and an open heart, ready and able to modify our plan according to the reality of the moment.

The mind also enjoys excursions into realms of fantasy, where it creates an internal video of a new and different me: famous, handsome, powerful, talented, successful, wealthy, and loved. The capacity of the human mind to fantasize is wonderful, the basis of all our creativity. It allows us to imagine new inventions, create new art and music, arrive at new scientific hypotheses, and make plans for everything from new buildings to new chapters of our lives. Unfortunately it can become an escape, an escape from whatever is uncomfortable about the present moment, an escape from the anxiety of not knowing what is actually moving toward us, an escape from the fear that the next moment (or hour or day or year) could bring us difficulties or even death. Incessant fantasizing and daydreaming are different from directed creativity. Creativity comes from resting the mind in neutral, allowing it to clear itself and provide a fresh canvas on which new ideas, equations, poems, melodies, or colorful strokes can appear.

When we allow the mind to rest in the present, full of what is actually happening right now, redirecting it away from repeated fruitless, energy-sapping excursions into the past, future, or fantasy realms, we are doing something very important. We are conserving the energy of the mind. It remains fresh and open, ready to respond to whatever appears before it.

This may sound trivial, but it is not.

Ordinarily our mind does not rest. Even at night it is active, generating dreams from a mix of anxieties and the events of our life. We know that our body cannot function well without rest, so we give it at least a few hours to lie down and relax each night. We forget, though, that our mind needs rest too. Where it finds rest is in the present moment, where it can lie down and relax into the flow of events.

Mindfulness practice reminds us not to fritter our mental energy away in trips to past and future, but to keep returning to this very place, to rest in what is happening in this very time.

2. Mindfulness trains and strengthens the mind

We are all aware that the human body can be trained. We can become more flexible (gymnasts and acrobats), more graceful (ballet dancers), more skilled (piano players), and stronger (weight lifters). We are less aware that there are many aspects of mind that can be cultivated. Just before his enlightenment the Buddha described the qualities of mind and heart that he had developed over many years. He observed that his mind had become "concentrated, purified, bright, unblemished, malleable, wieldy, rid of imperfections, imperturbable." When we practice mindfulness, we learn to lift the mind up out of its habitual preoccupations and place it down in a place of our choosing in order to illuminate some aspect of our life. We are training the mind to be light, powerful, and flexible but also able to concentrate on what we ask it to focus on.

The Buddha spoke of taming the mind. He said it was like taming a wild forest elephant. Just as an untamed elephant can do damage, trampling crops and injuring people, so the untamed, capricious mind can cause harm to us and those around us. Our human minds have a much larger capacity and power than we realize. Mindfulness is a potent tool for training the mind, allowing us to access and use the mind's true potential for insight, kindness, and creativity.

The Buddha pointed out that when a wild elephant is first captured and led out of the jungle, it has to be tethered to a stake. In the case of our mind, that stake takes the form of whatever we attend to in our mindfulness practice—for example, the breath, a mouthful of food, or our posture. We anchor the mind by returning it over and over to one thing. This calms the mind and rids it of distractions.

A wild elephant has many wild habits. It runs away when humans approach. It attacks when frightened. Our mind is similar. When it senses danger, it runs away from the present. It might run to pleasant fantasies, to thoughts of future revenge, or just go numb. If it is frightened, it may attack other people in an angry outburst, or it may attack inwardly, in silent but corrosive self-criticism.

In the time of the Buddha, elephants were trained to go into battle, to obey commands without fleeing from the din and chaos of war. Similarly, a mind trained through mindfulness can stand steady under the rapidly changing conditions of modern life. Once our mind is tamed, we can remain calm and stable as we encounter the inevitable difficulties the world brings us. Eventually we don't run from problems but see them as a way to test and strengthen our physical and mental stability.

Mindfulness helps us become aware of the mind's habitual and conditioned patterns of escape and allows us to try an alternative way of being in the world. That alternative is resting our awareness in the actual events of the present moment—the sounds heard by the ear, the sensations felt by the skin, the colors and shapes taken in by the eyes. Mindfulness helps stabilize the heart and mind so they are not so badly tossed around by the unexpected things that arrive in our life. If we practice mindfulness patiently and long enough, eventually we become interested in everything that happens, curious about what we can learn even from adversity and, eventually, even from our own death.

3. Mindfulness is good for the environment

Most of this mental activity, circling around endlessly in the realms of the past, future, and fantasy life, is not only pointless, it is destructive. How? It is fueled by an ecologically harmful fuel. That fuel is anxiety.

You might wonder, how is anxiety related to ecology? When we talk of ecology, we usually think of a world of physical relationships among living beings, such as the relationships among the bacteria, fungi, plants, and animals in a forest. But ecological relationships are based on energy exchange, and anxiety is an energy.

We might be aware that if a mother is chronically anxious, it could affect her unborn child adversely, through changes in blood flow and in the nutrients and hormones that bathe the baby. In the same way, when we are anxious, it affects the multitude of living "beings" inside us—our heart, our liver, our gut, the billions of bacteria in our gut, our skin. The negative effects of our fear and anxiety are not confined to the container of our body. Our anxiety also affects every being we come in contact with. Fear is a highly contagious state of mind, one that spreads quickly through families, communities, and whole nations.

Mindfulness involves resting our mind in a place where there is no anxiety, no fear. In fact, in that place we find the opposite. We discover resourcefulness, courage, and a quiet happiness.

Where is that "place"? It is not a geographic location. It is not a location in time. It is the flowing time and place of the present moment. Anxiety is fueled by thoughts of past and future. When we drop those thoughts, we drop anxiety and find ourselves at ease. How do we drop thoughts? We drop thoughts by temporarily withdrawing energy from the thinking function of the mind and redirecting it to the awareness function of the mind. This deliberate infusion of awareness is the essence of mindfulness. Relaxed, alert awareness is the antidote to anxiety and fear, both our own and others'. It is an ecologically beneficial way to live a human life; it changes the atmosphere for the better.

4. Mindfulness creates intimacy

Our essential hunger is not for food but for intimacy. When intimacy is missing in our lives, we feel isolated from other beings, alone, vulnerable, and unloved in the world.

We habitually look to other people to fulfill our needs for intimacy. However, our partners and friends cannot always be there for us in the way we need. Luckily a profound experience of intimacy is always accessible to us—all it requires is that we turn around and move toward life. This will require courage. We have to intentionally open our senses, becoming deliberately aware of what is going on both inside our body and heart/mind, and also outside, in our environment.

Mindfulness is a deceptively simple tool for helping us to be aware. It is a practice that helps us wake up, be present, and live life more abundantly. It helps fill in the gaps in our day, the many times we go unconscious and are not present for big chunks of our life. It is also a practice that will help us close the frustrating gap, the invisible shield that seems to exist between ourselves and other people.

5. Mindfulness stops our struggling and conquers fear

Mindfulness helps us stay present with experiences that aren't pleasant. Our usual tendency is to try to arrange the world and other people so that we are comfortable. We spend a lot of energy trying to make the temperature around us just right, the lighting just right, the fragrance in the air just right, the food just right, our beds and chairs just the right softness, the colors of our walls just right, the grounds around our homes just right, and the people around us—our children, intimate partners, friends, coworkers, and even pets—just right.

But, try as we might, things don't stay the way we want them to. Sooner or later, our child throws a tantrum, dinner burns, the heating system breaks down, we become ill. If we are able to stay present and open, even to welcome experiences and people that aren't comfortable for us, they will lose their power to frighten us and make us react or flee. If we can do this over and over again, we will have gained an amazing power, rare in the human world—to be happy despite constantly changing conditions.

6. Mindfulness supports our spiritual life

Mindfulness tools are an invitation to bring attention to the many small activities of life. They are particularly helpful to people who would like to nurture a spiritual life in the midst of all the distractions of modern living. Zen Master Suzuki Roshi said, "Zen is not some kind of excitement, but concentration on our usual everyday routine." Mindfulness practice brings our awareness back to this body, this time, this place. This is exactly where we can be touched by the eternal presence we call the Divine. When we are mindful, we are appreciating each moment of the particular life we have been given. Mindfulness is a way of expressing our gratitude for a gift that we can never repay. Mindfulness can become a constant prayer of gratitude.

Christian mystics speak of a "life of continuous prayer." What could this mean? How could it be possible when we are swept along in the speedy traffic of modern life, cutting corners continuously, without enough time to talk to our own family, let alone God?

True prayer is not petitioning, it is listening. Deep listening. When we listen deeply, we find that even the "sound" of our own thoughts is disruptive, even annoying. Letting go of thoughts, we enter a more profound inner stillness and receptivity. If this open silence can be held at our core, as our core, then we are no longer confused by trying to sort out and choose among our myriad competing inner voices. Our attention is no longer caught up in the emotional tangle within. It is directed outward. We are looking for the Divine in all appearances, listening to the Divine in all sounds, brushed by the Divine in all touches. As things move toward us, we respond appropriately, and then return to resting in inner silence. This is a life lived in faith, faith in the One Mind, a life of continuous prayer.

When we infuse one routine activity with mindfulness, then another, and another, we are waking up to the mystery of each moment, unknowable until it arrives. As things come forward, we are ready to receive and respond. We are receptive to what is being given to us, moment by moment, by the Great Presence. They are simple gifts: warmth spreading through our hands as we hold a cup of tea, thousands of tiny caresses as clothing touches our skin, the complex music of raindrops, one more breath. When we are able to give full attention to the living truth of each moment, we enter the gate to a life of continuous prayer.

Misunderstandings about Mindfulness

Although mindfulness is highly touted, people may easily misunderstand it. First, they may mistakenly believe that to practice mindfulness means to think hard about something. In mindfulness we use the thinking power of the mind only to initiate the practice ("Be aware of your posture today") and to remind us to return to the practice when the mind inevitably wanders during the day

("Return your awareness to your posture"). However, once we follow the mind's instructions and begin to use the method, we can let go of thoughts. When the thinking mind quiets down, it shifts into open awareness. Then we are anchored in the body, alert and present.

The second misunderstanding about mindfulness is that it means doing everything *very slowly*. The speed at which we do things is not the point. It is possible to perform a task slowly and still be inattentive. Actually, when we move faster, we often need to become more attentive if we want to avoid errors. To use some of the mindfulness tools in this book, you may need to slow down—for example, while practicing mindful eating. For other exercises you will be asked to slow down briefly, to bring the mind and body together before reengaging with your regular activities— for example, resting the mind for three breaths. Other tasks can be done at any speed, such as the exercise that involves paying attention to the bottoms of the feet while sitting, walking, or running.

A third common misunderstanding is to think of mindfulness as a program of time-limited exercises, such as a thirty-minute period of sitting meditation. Mindfulness is helpful to the extent that it spreads out into all the activities of our life, bringing the light of heightened awareness, curiosity, and a sense of discovery to the mundane activities of life, like getting up in the morning, brushing teeth, walking through a door, answering a phone, listening to someone talk.

How to Use This Book

This book offers a wide variety of ways to bring mindfulness into your daily life. We call them "mindfulness exercises." You could also think of them as mindfulness "seeds," seeds to plant and grow mindfulness in the many nooks and corners of your life, seeds you can watch as they grow and bear fruit each day.

Each exercise has several sections. First there is a description of the task and some ideas about how to remind yourself to do it throughout the day and week. Next is a section titled "Discoveries," which includes people's observations, insights, or difficulties with the task, along with any relevant research findings. In the section called "Deeper

Lessons" I explore the themes and larger life lessons connected with the exercise. Each exercise is like a window, giving us a glimpse of what an awakened life would be like. Lastly there are a few "Final Words," which sum up the exercise or inspire you to continue letting it unfold.

One way to use the book is to start each week by reading only the description of the task and how to remind yourself to do it. No peeking ahead! Post your reminder words or pictures where you'll see them during the day in order to remember the task. Midweek you could read the Discoveries section for that particular exercise to see what experiences and insights other people have had in trying it. This might change how you approach the exercise. At the end of the week you could read the Deeper Lessons section before moving on to a new exercise.

You might want to do what we do at the monastery: we begin with the first mindfulness exercise and move through the year in order, practicing each exercise for one week. You could start a new one each Monday and finish reading or journaling about it on the following Sunday. You can also skip around if a specific exercise or theme seems suited to the conditions of your life this week. Sometimes we continue trying the same mindfulness practice for two or three weeks if it continues to yield insights or we'd like to get better at doing it.

It's fun to do these practices with other people, as we do at the monastery. You might form a mindfulness practice group that picks an exercise to use for a week or two and then meets so that people can share what they've learned. There's a lot of laughter at our weekly discussions. It's important to take our "failures" lightly. Each person has different experiences, insights, and funny stories to tell about his or her attempts—and failures—to do these exercises.

We began the practice of taking on a new mindfulness tool or task each week at the monastery about twenty years ago. The idea came from a man who had lived in a community that followed the teachings of the mystic G. I. Gurdjieff. He explained that it didn't matter if you succeeded with the task or not. Sometimes *not doing* the exercise could teach you more than doing it, because you got to look at why you didn't do it. What was behind it—

laziness, old aversions, or just spacing out? The point is to live more and more in a conscious way. Gurdjieff called this "self-remembering." In Buddhism we call it awakening to our true self. It is waking up to our life as it actually is, not to the fantasy we often live out in our mind.

Reminders

Over the years we have found that the most difficult part of our weekly mindfulness practices is just remembering to do them. So we've invented various ways to remind ourselves throughout the day and week. Often we stick words or small images up around the monastery where we are likely to encounter them. You can see sample reminders at www.shambhala.com/howtotrain, but please be creative and invent your own.

A Mindfulness Practice Notebook

To help you get the most out of these practices, I recommend using a notebook to record what you experience and learn as you work with each mindfulness exercise. If you're working through the book with a group, you can bring the notebook to your discussion sessions to remind you about the discoveries you made and the obstacles you encountered. Having a notebook on your desk or bedside table also helps as a reminder to do the practice of the week.

Continuing on

We hope that once we use a mindfulness tool for a week, it will stick with us and become part of our ever-expanding capacity for mindfulness. Being human, however, we often lapse back into old behaviors and unconscious habit patterns. That is why at the monastery we have continued to use these mindfulness practices for two decades, and to invent new ones. This is one of the most wonderful aspects of the path of mindfulness and awakening. It has no end!

I

Use Your Nondominant Hand

THE EXERCISE: Use your nondominant hand for some ordinary tasks each day. These could include brushing your teeth, combing your hair, or eating with the nondominant hand for at least part of each meal. If you're up for a big challenge, try using the nondominant hand when writing or when eating with chopsticks.

Reminding Yourself

One way to remember this task throughout your day is to put a Band-Aid on your dominant hand. When you notice it, switch hands and use the nondominant hand. You could also tape a small sign on your bathroom mirror that says "Left Hand" (if you're right-handed). Or tape a paper cutout of a hand to your mirror, refrigerator, or desk—wherever you're likely to see it.

Another approach is to tape something to the handle of your toothbrush, reminding you to brush your teeth with the nondominant hand.

Discoveries

This experiment always evokes laughter. We discover that the nondominant hand is quite clumsy. Using it brings us back to what Zen teachers call "beginner's mind." Our dominant hand might be forty years old, but the nondominant hand is much younger, perhaps about two or three years old. We have to learn all over again how to hold a fork and how to get it into our mouths without stabbing ourselves. We might begin to brush our teeth very awkwardly with the nondominant hand, and when we aren't looking our dominant hand will reach out and take the toothbrush or fork away! It is just like a bossy older sister who says, "Hey, you little klutz, let me do it for you!"

Struggling to use the nondominant hand can awaken our compassion for anyone who is clumsy or unskilled, such as a person who has had disabilities, injuries, or a stroke. We briefly see how much we take for granted scores of simple movements that many people cannot make. Using chopsticks with the nondominant hand is a humbling experience. If you want to eat a meal in under an hour and not end up spilling food all over, you have to be very attentive.

Deeper Lessons

This task illustrates how strong and unconscious our habits are and how difficult they are to change without awareness and determination. This task helps us bring beginner's mind to any activity—such as eating—that we do several times a day, often with only partial awareness.

Using the nondominant hand reveals our impatience. It can help us become more flexible and discover that we are never too old to learn new tricks. If we practice using the nondominant hand frequently, over time we can watch our skill develop. I have been practicing using my left hand for several years and I now forget which hand is the "right" hand to use. This could have practical benefits. If I lose the use of my dominant hand, as a number of my relatives did after strokes, I won't be "left" helpless. When we develop a new skill, we realize that there are many other abilities lying dormant within us. This insight can arouse confidence that, with practice, we can transform ourselves in many ways, moving toward more flexibility and freedom in life. If we are willing to make the effort, over time we can awaken the skills arising from the natural wisdom within us and let them function in our daily life.

Zen Master Suzuki Roshi said, "In the beginner's mind there are many possibilities, but in the expert's there are few." Mindfulness enables us to keep returning to the unlimited possibilities that are always emerging from the great birthing place of the present moment.

FINAL WORDS: To bring possibilities into your life, unfold beginner's mind in all situations.

2

Filler Words

THE EXERCISE: Become aware of the use of "filler" words and phrases, and try to eliminate them from your speech. Fillers are words that do not add meaning to what you're saying, such as "um," "ah," "so," "well," "like," "you know," "kind of," and "sort of." Additional filler words enter our vocabulary from time to time. Recent additions might include "basically" and "anyway."

In addition to eliminating filler

words, see if you can notice why you tend to use them—in what situations and for what purpose?

Reminding Yourself

It is mortifyingly difficult to notice yourself using filler words at first. You will probably have to enlist the help of friends or family members. Children will love catching and correcting their parents using filler words. Ask them to raise their hands when they hear you use a filler word. At first, hands will pop up and down with annoying frequency, and so unconscious is this habit that you may have to ask them to tell you what filler word you just uttered!

Another way to be able to hear the filler words you use and their frequency is to record yourself talking. Ask a roommate, spouse, or child to use his or her cell phone or video camera to record you in conversation or while you're talking on the phone. Play it back and tabulate the fillers you use and their frequency.

Discoveries

At the monastery we have found this to be one of the most challenging mindfulness practices we do. It is frustratingly hard to hear your own filler words and catch them before they are spoken—unless you are a trained speaker. In the Toastmasters clubs (groups that train in public speaking) there are people assigned to tally filler words during talks, assisting members as they learn to be effective speakers. Once you begin to hear filler words, you will hear them everywhere, on the radio and TV and in everyday conversation. A typical teenager uses the filler word *like* an estimated two hundred thousand times a year! You will also notice which speakers do not use them and become aware of how the absence of filler words makes a speech more effective and powerful. For example, listen to Martin Luther King Jr., the Dalai Lama, or President Barack Obama's speeches with an ear for filler words.

Filler words seem to serve several functions. They are space holders, telling the listener that you are going to start speaking or that you are not finished speaking yet. "So . . . I told him what I thought of his idea and then, um, I said, like, you know . . ." Filler words also soften what we say, making it less definite or assertive. "So anyway, I, you know, think we should, basically, kind of go ahead with this project." Are we afraid of provoking a reaction or of being wrong? We wouldn't want a president or doctor who spoke in such a wishy-washy way. Filler words can become an obstruction to the listening audience when they so dilute the meaning as to render it silly. "Jesus sort of said, 'Love your, you know, neighbor, as, sort of, like, yourself.'"

Deeper Lessons

Filler words have become common only in the last fifty years. Is this because there is less emphasis in schools on precise speech, elocution, and good debating skills? Or, in today's multicultural, postmodern world, where truth is often regarded as relative, have we purposely moved to speaking in less definitive ways? Are we afraid to say something that might be politically incorrect or provoke a reaction from our audience? Are we sinking into moral relativism? If this trend continues, we will find ourselves saying, "Stealing is like, sort of, in a way, wrong."

When our mind is clear, we can speak in a straightforward way, with precision, and without insulting others.

This mindfulness tool shows how entrenched unconscious behaviors are, and how difficult they are to change. Unconscious habits such as using filler words are just that: unconscious. As long as they remain unconscious, they are impossible to change. Only when we bring the light of awareness to a pattern of behavior do we begin to have some space to work to modify them. Even then, it is very difficult to change an ingrained behavior. As soon as we stop working actively to change an unwanted habit, it quickly returns. If we want to change ourselves, if we want to realize our potential, it takes kindness, determination, and steady, sustained practice.

FINAL WORDS: "I think you're all enlightened until you open your mouths."—Zen Master Suzuki Roshi

---

3

Appreciate Your Hands

THE EXERCISE: Several times a day, when your hands are busy, watch them as though they belonged to a stranger. Also look at them when they are still.

Reminding Yourself

Write the words "Watch Me" on the back of your hand.

If your work makes this impossible, put on a ring that you don't usually wear. (If you are not allowed to wear rings, say because you work in an operating room, you can use the time of hand washing or putting on surgical gloves to become aware of your hands as though they belonged to a stranger.)

If you don't usually wear nail polish, you could remind yourself to watch your hands by painting your nails for a week. Or, if you do wear polish, you could wear an unusual color.

Discoveries

Our hands are very skilled at all sorts of tasks, and they can do many of them by themselves, without much direction from our mind. It's fun to watch them at work, busily living their own life. Hands can do so much! The two hands can work together or do different things at the same time.

While doing this exercise we noticed

that each person has characteristic hand gestures. Our hands wave about when we talk, almost by themselves. We noticed that our hands change over time. Look at your hands and imagine them as they were when you were a baby, then imagine them changing as you grew older, until they reach the present time and state. Then imagine them growing older, becoming lifeless when you die, then dissolving back into the earth.

Even when we are asleep our hands are caring for us—pulling up the blankets, holding the body next to us, turning off the alarm clock.

Deeper Lessons

We are being taken care of all the time. Some Zen teachers say that the way the body takes care of us, without our even being aware of it, is an example of the beautiful and continuous functioning of our Original Nature, the inherent goodness and wisdom of our being. Our hand pulls back from fire before we even register heat, our eyes blink before we are aware of a sharp sound, our hand reaches out to catch something before we know it is falling. The right and left hands work together, each one doing its half of a task. Drying dishes, one hand holds the dish and the other the towel. Cutting with a knife, one holds the vegetable while the other chops. They cooperate to wash each other.

There is a koan (a Zen teaching story) about the bodhisattva of compassion, who is called Kanzeon in Japanese, Kuan Yin in Chinese. She is often depicted with a thousand eyes, to see every person in need of comfort, and a thousand hands, each holding a different implement to aid them. Sometimes there is even an eye in the palm of each hand. The story is this:

> One day the Zen monk Ungan asked Zen Master Dogo, "How does the Bodhisattva Kanzeon use all those many hands and eyes?"
>
> Dogo answered, "It is like a man in the middle of the night reaching behind his head for his pillow."

One of my students is a luthier, and he had insight into this story. Working inside the body of a guitar on a spot he could not see, he realized that his hands have "eyes." They can "see" the surface they are touching, in detail, and work on it, even in the dark. His inner eye and his hand were working together beautifully, just as a sleeping man "sees" his pillow and his hands naturally reach out to pull it under his head. In Zen we say this shows the way our innate wisdom and compassion work together when our mind is not in the way.

When we see clearly into the unity of all existence, we see that all things are working together, like the hands and eyes. As our hands would not hurt our eyes, our nature is to not hurt ourselves or each other.

FINAL WORDS: The two hands work together effortlessly to accomplish many wonderful things, and they never harm each other. Could this become true for any two human beings?

4

When Eating, Just Eat

THE EXERCISE: This week, when you're eating or drinking, don't do anything else. Sit down and take the time to enjoy what you are taking in. Open all the senses as you eat or drink. Look at the colors, shapes, surface textures. Attend to the smells and flavors in your mouth. Listen to the sounds of eating and drinking.

Reminding Yourself

Post a note on the table where you eat meals that says, "Just Eat." Also post this note wherever you are likely to snack.

Also post notes on objects that tend to distract you while you eat. For example, on your computer or TV, post the word "Eating" with an X through it as a reminder to not eat while using it.

Discoveries

This is not an easy task for most people. If you're on the go, walking from one place to another, and about to take a sip of tea or coffee, you're going to need to stop, find a place to sit down, and savor it. If you're working on the computer, you're going to have to take both hands off the keyboard and turn your eyes away from the screen in order to savor a sip of coffee.

Eating has become part of our modern habit of perpetually multitasking. When we do this exercise, we discover anew how many other things we do while eating. We eat while walking, driving, watching TV or movies, reading, working on the computer, playing video games, and listening to music.

Once we eliminate those obvious activities, we come to a more subtle aspect of inattention—talking while eating. Our parents may have scolded us for talking with our mouths full, but we still find ourselves eating and talking simultaneously. While doing this task we learn to alternate eating and talking. In other words, if you want to talk, stop eating. Don't do them at the same time.

It is so common to socialize while

eating that you may discover that you feel awkward eating alone in a restaurant without reading or otherwise distracting yourself. You might imagine that people are thinking, "Poor thing, no friends." You pick up a book or open your computer to show you are being productive and wouldn't "waste time" by "just eating." One problem with eating and doing other things is that it becomes "waist time"—that is, time for extra food to go down unnoticed and end up on your waist!

In Japan and parts of Europe it is very rude to walk and eat or drink at the same time. The only food you can eat in Japan while standing up or walking is an ice-cream cone, because it might melt. People will stare at the boorish foreigner who buys fast food and walks down the street munching.

Even fast food is taken home, arranged attractively, and served at a table. Meals are times to slow down and truly enjoy the food, drink, and company.

Deeper Lessons

Why do we feel compelled to multitask, to not waste time by just eating? It seems that our self-worth is based on how much we can produce in a day, or how many items we can cross off our long "to do" list. Eating and drinking are activities that don't earn us money, a spouse, or a Nobel Prize, so we begin to think they have no value. During mindful-eating workshops many people say, "Oh, I just eat to get it over with so I can get on with my work." What if the most important work we do each day is to be truly present, even for only thirty minutes? What if the most important gift we can give to the world is not any kind of product or present but is, instead, our presence?

When we are not paying attention, it is as if the food did not exist. We can clean our plate and still feel dissatisfied. We will keep on eating, stopping only when we are over-full and uncomfortable. If we eat with mindful awareness, then the experience of eating even one bite becomes rich and varied. Then we can eat until we feel inner satisfaction rather than eating until we feel stuffed.

The Zen monk Thich Nhat Hanh writes,

> There are some people who eat an orange but don't really eat it. They eat their sorrow, fear, anger; their past and future. They are not really present, with body and mind united.

> You need some training just to enjoy [your food]. It has come from the whole cosmos just for our nourishment . . . this is a miracle.

FINAL WORDS: When eating, just eat. When drinking, just drink. Mindfulness is the very best seasoning, for your food and for your entire life. Enjoy each bite, enjoy each moment!

5

True Compliments

THE EXERCISE: Once a day, think of someone close to you—a family member, a friend, or a coworker—and give them a genuine compliment. The closer the person is to you, the better, such as a child or a parent. (It doesn't count to tell a stranger at the post office that you like their scarf.) The more specific the compliment, the better. "I appreciate the way you answer the phone so cheerfully."

Become aware also of any compliments other people give you. Investigate the purpose of compliments and the effect on you of being given a compliment.

Reminding Yourself

Post the word "Praise" or "Compliment" in places where you'll see it throughout the day.

Discoveries

Some people report that they were resistant to this task at first, because they feared their compliments wouldn't be genuine. They soon discovered many things they could be grateful for, and they were able to do the exercise. Some people realized as they did this task that they have a habitual stance that is critical, only noticing and remarking on problems. Undertaking this practice helped highlight and reverse this state of mind.

Other people commented that when they gave compliments, they noticed that the person receiving the compliment often blocked it. "Oh, I don't think my cookies are so good this time." Being given a compliment creates vulnerability. Some people may have become wary of compliments in adolescence, when they couldn't be sure if a compliment was meant sincerely or was designed to make them the butt of a joke. Perhaps they also began to give compliments in a joking way or to rebut a compliment as if it were a joke in order to protect themselves from potential embarrassment. One person reported that his parents had to teach him how to receive compliments. They advised, "Simply say, 'Thank you.' That's all the other person needs."

Another man described how he had actively studied the art of giving compliments because he had never been given anything but negative feedback when he was growing up in an alcoholic home. He found that giving compliments "lightens things up and shifts the energy to positive." He also found that his children, spouse, and employees seem to thrive when given genuine compliments.

There are some cultural differences in how compliments are received. In studies in China and Japan, 95 percent of responses to compliments were designed to deny or deflect the praise. In

Asia it is normal to dismiss or back away from compliments, because one might be seen to lack humility. A husband would not compliment his wife in front of others, lest it seem that he is bragging.

Nonviolent Communication, an approach to effective conflict resolution, teaches that a compliment such as "You're so [adjective] . . ." tends to be disconnecting. They recommend centering compliments around something that touched you, because this type of compliment promotes a sense of connection and intimacy. "I was touched by how you took the time to bake fresh cookies for this meeting. Thank you."

This mindfulness exercise helps us become aware of the function and frequency of compliments in our relationships with others. Some compliments seem genuine while others seem aimed at getting something in return. When we first meet someone, or when we are courting, more compliments are exchanged. Later we seem to take those close to us for granted and stop expressing praise, gratitude, or appreciation.

Deeper Lessons

Zen Master Dogen wrote, "You should know that kind speech arises from kind mind, and kind mind from the seed of compassionate mind. You should ponder the fact that kind speech is not just praising the merit of others; it has the power to turn the destiny of the nation."

The Buddhist teachings describe three feeling tones we experience in reaction to people, objects, or events:

positive (a happy feeling), negative (an irritated feeling), and neutral (no positive or negative feelings). When we feel positively about a person, we are more likely to beam a positive feeling tone toward them and to give them compliments. For example, we're naturally inclined to compliment someone we are courting or a cute baby who hasn't yet transformed into an obstinate toddler.

When someone becomes part of the furniture of our life, we forget to notice what they do and it doesn't occur to us to give them compliments. In fact, we may only comment on the negative, the things we see that we think need to be changed. Without our intending it, this can gradually impart a negative feeling tone to the entire relationship.

The practice of actively noticing what a person does well and giving genuine compliments can add new warmth, intimacy, and responsiveness to a relationship.

Personal compliments about temporary or conditional qualities such as beauty make us a little uncomfortable. Why is this? Because we intuitively know that some qualities, such as physical beauty, are serendipitous intersections of genes and current cultural norms. We did not sculpt our handsome face. It is a temporary gift. We know that with time it will change into something with a double chin and many wrinkles. In even a year's time it could become defined as "ugly." Straight hair becomes popular for a few years, and girls with curly hair spend hours straightening it. Then curly hair comes into fashion. Most of the things we get compliments for are temporary—a slim figure, athletic ability, even intelligence. They are seldom qualities that we actually earned. This is why the best compliments are founded upon appreciation for how a person made you feel.

Below the temporary qualities that garner compliments lies our True Nature. In Buddhism this is called our Buddha nature; in other religions it is called our divine nature. It is our essence. It is not based on feelings, physical characteristics, or any kind of comparison. It cannot be inflated by compliments or diminished by criticism. There is nothing you do that can add to it, nothing you do that can subtract from it. No matter what you have done wrong or right, no matter what has been done to you, it remains untouched. It does not increase when you are born or decrease when you die. It is the Eternal expressing itself as you.

FINAL WORDS: Kind words are a gift. They create wealth in the heart.

6

Listen to Sounds

THE EXERCISE: Several times a day, stop and just listen. Open your hearing 360 degrees, as if your ears were giant radar dishes. Listen to the obvious sounds and the subtle sounds—in your body, in the room, in the building, and outside. Listen as if you had just landed from a foreign planet and didn't know what was making these sounds. See if you can hear all sounds as music being played just for you.

Reminding Yourself

Post a simple drawing of an ear in various places in your home and workplace.

Discoveries

We are continuously bathed in sound, even in places we would call quiet, such as libraries or forests. Our ears register all these sounds, but our brain blocks most of them out so that we can concentrate on the important ones—the conversation, the lecture, the radio program, the airplane engine, and is that the baby crying?

Research indicates that babies can hear things adults cannot. Their hearing is acute enough to detect the subtle echoes that occur after most sounds. We learn early in life to block these confusing sounds out. Interestingly, African Bushmen retain this ability, probably because they live in the very quiet environment of the desert. Babies also recognize music and the melodic qualities of the voices they heard before birth.

When we begin listening carefully, a new world opens up. Sounds that were annoying become interesting and even amusing when we hear them as some kind of alien music. Background noise moves into the foreground. We discover a lot of noise in our mouth when we eat, especially crunchy food. The neighbor's leaf blower becomes part of the ongoing symphony of sounds. A jackhammer is the percussion section. The hum of the refrigerator unfolds into a tapestry of many subtle high and low notes.

Deeper Lessons

Listening practice is a potent way to quiet the mind. When we become intrigued by sounds, we want to listen more closely. To listen intently, we have to ask the voices in the mind to be quiet for a while. We have to ask the mind not to name ("John's old truck") or talk about the sounds ("He needs a new muffler") but just to be alert and to listen, as if we were hearing each sound for the first time. In fact, we are. Each sound is just that: completely new.

Listening is an excellent way to disengage from the endless ruminations of the anxious mind. As soon as you find your mind spinning in a squirrel cage of its own making, stop and listen to the music of the room. When you are frazzled after spending an entire day on your computer, step outside, open your awareness out into the darkness, and listen to the music of the evening.

There is a famous koan about sound. A koan is a question for opening the mind into a direct experience of deeper reality. The eminent Japanese Zen master Hakuin assigned his students the koan, "What is the sound of one hand?" It has become trivialized in modern times (and incorrectly repeated as "What is the sound of one hand clapping?"), but when it is taken on with all earnestness, it can open the mind into profound listening.

Reduce this koan to its essence: "What is the sound?" or just "Sound?" When your mind has wandered away down its endless twisting corridors, let this question bring it back to here and now.

FINAL WORDS: Even in what is called silence there is sound. To hear such subtle sound, the mind must be very quiet.

7

Loving Touch

THE EXERCISE: Use loving hands and a loving touch, even with inanimate objects.

Reminding Yourself

Put something unusual on a finger of your dominant hand. Some possibilities include a different ring, a Band-Aid, a dot of nail polish on one nail, or a small mark made with a colored pen. Each time you notice the marker, remember to use loving hands, loving touch.

Discoveries

When we do this practice, we soon become aware of when we or others are *not* using loving hands. We notice how groceries are thrown into the shopping cart, luggage is hurled onto a conveyor belt at the airport, and silverware is tossed into a bin. We hear metal bowls singing out when stacked carelessly and doors slamming when we rush.

A particular dilemma arose at our monastery for people who were weeding the garden. How can we practice loving hands when we are pulling a living plant out of the ground by its roots? Can we keep our heart open to it, placing it in the compost with a prayer that its life (and ours) will benefit others?

As a medical student, I worked with a number of surgeons who were known for their "surgical temperament." If any difficulty arose during an operation, they would act like two-year-olds, throwing expensive instruments and cursing at nurses. I noticed that one surgeon was different. He remained calm under stress, but more importantly, he handled the tissue of each unconscious patient as if it were precious. I resolved that if I needed surgery, I would insist he do it.

As we do this practice, mindfulness of loving touch expands to include awareness not just of how we touch things but awareness also of how we are touched. This includes not just how we are touched by human hands but also how we are touched by our clothing, the wind, the food and drink in our mouth, the floor under our feet, and many other things.

We know how to use loving hands and touch. We touch babies, faithful dogs, crying children, and lovers with tenderness and care. Why don't we use loving touch all the time? This is the essential question of mindfulness. Why can't I live like this all the time? Once we discover how much richer our life is when we are more present, why do we fall back into our old habits and space out?

Deeper Lessons

We are being touched all the time, but we are largely unaware of it. Touch usually enters our awareness only when it is uncomfortable (a rock in my sandal) or associated with intense desire (when she or he kisses me for the first time). When we begin to open our awareness to all the touch sensations, both inside and outside our bodies, we might feel frightened. It can be overwhelming.

Ordinarily we are more aware of using loving touch with people than with objects. However, when we are in a hurry or upset with someone, we turn him or her into an object. We rush out of the house without saying good-bye to someone we love, we ignore a coworker's greeting because of a disagreement the day before. This is how other people become objectified, a nuisance, an obstacle, and ultimately, an enemy.

In Japan objects are often personified. Many things are honored and treated with loving care, things we would consider inanimate and therefore not deserving of respect, let alone love. Money is handed to cashiers with two hands, tea whisks are given personal names, broken sewing needles are given a funeral and laid to rest in a soft block of tofu, the honorific "o-" is attached to mundane things such as money (*o-kane*), water (*o-mizu*), tea (*o-cha*), and even chopsticks (*o-hashi*). This may come from the Shinto tradition of honoring the *kami* or spirits that reside in waterfalls, large trees, and mountains. If water, wood, and stone are seen as holy, then all things that arise from them are also holy.

My Zen teachers taught me, through example, how to handle all things as if they were alive. Zen Master Maezumi Roshi opened envelopes, even junk mail, using a letter opener in order to make a clean cut, and removed the contents with careful attention. He became upset when people used their feet to drag meditation cushions around the floor or banged their plates down on the table. “I can feel it in my body,” he once said. While most modern priests use clothes hangers, Zen Master Harada Roshi takes time to fold his monk’s robes each night and to “press” them under his mattress or suitcase. His everyday robe is always crisp. There are robes hundreds of years old in his care. He treats each robe as the robe of the Buddha.

Can we imagine the touch-awareness of enlightened beings? How sensitive and how wide might their field of awareness be? Jesus became immediately aware when a sick woman touched the hem of his garment and was healed.

FINAL WORDS: "When you handle rice, water, or anything else, have the affectionate and caring concern of a parent raising a child." —Zen Master Dogen

8

Waiting

THE EXERCISE: Any time you find yourself waiting—when you're in line at the store, waiting for someone who's late, or waiting for the "please wait" icon on your computer screen to go away—take this as an opportunity to practice mindfulness, meditation, or prayer.

There are several good mindfulness practices for waiting time. One is mindfulness of breath, beginning with a few deep breaths to help dispel body tension over having to wait or the possibility of someone you are waiting for being late. Find the place in your body where you are most aware of the breath—nostrils, chest, or belly—and put your attention on the sensations in that area, noticing how they are continuously changing.

Another useful practice for waiting time is listening to sounds, opening and expanding your hearing to take in the whole room. Other good practices include loving-kindness for the body and relaxing on the out-breath: each time you breathe out, notice any extra holding or tension in the body—around the eyes or mouth, in the shoulders or belly—and let it soften.

When you notice yourself becoming annoyed by having to wait, remind yourself, "This is terrific! I have some unexpected time to practice mindfulness."

Reminding Yourself

Put a small note or piece of tape with the letter W (for "waiting practice") on the timing devices you check throughout the day, such as your watch, the clock in your car, or your cell phone. Also put a W on your computer screen or mouse.

Discoveries

I discovered this practice when I was new to meditation, working seventy-two-hour weeks as an intern at a busy county hospital, with barely enough time to go to the bathroom. Two Zen teachers came by to visit me at the hospital. I hurried into the waiting room, murmuring apologies for keeping them waiting. "No problem," one said. "It gave us some extra time to sit." ("Sit" is Zen slang for doing sitting meditation.) Oh, yes.

This practice answers the question "When can I—a very busy person—find time to practice mindfulness?" We don't need to dedicate a large block of time to mindfulness practice (though that certainly doesn't hurt). Opportunities to practice being present arise throughout the day.

When we are forced to wait, say in a traffic jam, our instinct is to do something to distract ourselves from the discomfort of waiting. We turn on the radio, call or text someone on the phone, or just sit and fume. Practicing mindfulness while waiting helps people find many small moments in the day when they can bring the thread of awareness up from where it lies hidden in the complex fabric of their lives. Waiting, a common event that usually produces negative emotions, can be transformed into a gift, the gift of free time to practice. The mind benefits doubly: first, by abandoning negative mind-states, and second, by gaining the beneficial effects of even a few extra minutes of practice woven into the day.

My original "waiting practice" teacher was my very patient father. On Sunday morning he would don a suit and tie, and then get into the car to read the Sunday paper. Meanwhile his wife and three daughters would get into the car, one by one, and then get out again to run back and forth on many trips to retrieve gloves, pocketbooks, lipsticks, socks without holes, barrettes, Sunday school books, and so on. Only when the running and slamming of doors ceased would he look up, calmly fold the paper, and start the engine.

Deeper Lessons

As you undertake this practice, you learn to recognize early the body changes that accompany impending negative thoughts and emotions such as impatience about having to wait, or anger about "that idiot" ahead of us in the checkout line. Each time we are able to stop and not allow a negative mind-state to come to fruition (say, getting irritated at the traffic or angry at the slow cashier), we are erasing a habitual and unwholesome pattern of the heart/mind. If we don't let the cart of the mind keep running down the same deep ruts, down the same old hill, into the same old swamp, eventually the ruts will fill in. Eventually our habitual states of irritation and frustration over something like waiting will dissolve. It takes time, but it works. And it's worth it, as everyone around us will benefit.

Many of us have a mind that measures self-worth in terms of productivity. If I did not produce anything today, if I did not write a book, give a speech, bake bread, earn money, sell something, buy something, get a good grade on a test, or find my soul mate, then my day was wasted and I am a failure. We give ourselves no credit for taking "being" time, for just being present. "Waiting" is thus a source of frustration. Think of the things I could be getting done!

And yet, if you asked the people you care about what they would like most from you, their answer is likely to be some version of "your presence" or "your loving attention." Presence has no measurable product except positive feelings, feelings of support, intimacy, and happiness. When we stop being busy and productive and switch to just being still and aware, we ourselves will also feel support, intimacy, and happiness, even if no one else is around. These positive feelings are a "product" that is much desired but that cannot be bought. They are the natural result of presence. They are a birthright that we have forgotten we have.

FINAL WORDS: Don't be annoyed when you have to wait; rejoice in extra time to practice being present.

9

Secret Acts of Virtue

THE EXERCISE: Each day for a week, engage in a secret act of virtue or kindness. Do something nice or needed for others, but do so anonymously. These acts can be very simple, like washing someone else's dishes that were left in the sink, picking up trash on the sidewalk, cleaning the bathroom sink (when it's not your job), making an anonymous donation, or leaving a chocolate on a coworker's desk.

Reminding Yourself

Place a notebook on your bedside table and use it to make a plan each night for what your secret act of virtue will be the next day. You could also post little pictures of elves in strategic places in your home or workplace as reminders.

Discoveries

It's unexpectedly fun to plan and do nice things in secret for others. Once you take on this task in earnest, you begin looking around for new ideas, and the possibilities begin to multiply. "Oh, tomorrow I could have a cup of hot tea waiting on her desk, or I could clean the mud off his running shoes on the porch." It's like being a superhero named Secret Virtue, who, in the dark of night, creeps about doing good deeds. There's the excitement of trying not to get caught, and, as some people admitted, there can also be a bit of disappointment at not being caught or acknowledged. Even more interesting is remaining silent as someone else is thanked for the gift we gave anonymously.

All religions value generosity. The Bible says it is more blessed to give than to receive. There are two forms of charity in Islam: obligatory giving to take care of the poor and orphaned, and voluntary giving, such as endowments or scholarships. Obligatory giving purifies the rest of one's earnings and is considered a form of prayer or worship. Voluntary giving in secret is said to have seventy times the value of public giving.

One of my favorite practices is what I call "drive-by metta." (*Metta* is a Pali word meaning loving-kindness, or unconditional friendliness. It also refers to a meditative practice for developing those qualities.) As I drive to work, for each person I pass on the road—pedestrians, bikers, and especially rude drivers who are in a hurry—I say quietly, with my out-breath, "May you be free from anxiety. May you be at ease." I don't know if this secret practice helps them, but it definitely helps me. The days I do drive-by metta always go more easily.

Deeper Lessons

Our personality is cobbled together out of many strategies for making others love and care for us, for getting what we want, and for keeping ourselves safe.

We bask in positive recognition, for it signals love, success, and security. This task helps us look at how willing we are to put the effort out to do good things for others if we never earn credit for it. Zen practice emphasizes "going straight on"—leading our lives in a straightforward way based on what we know to be good practice, undaunted by praise or criticism.

A monk once asked the Chinese Zen master Hui-hai, "What is the gate [meaning both entrance and pillar] of Zen practice?" Hui-hai answered, "Complete giving."

The Buddha said, "If people knew, as I know, the fruits of sharing gifts, they would not enjoy their use without sharing them, nor would the taint of stinginess obsess the heart. Even if it were their last bit, their last morsel of food, they would not enjoy its use without sharing it if there was someone else to share it with."

The Buddha spoke constantly of the value of generosity, saying it is the most effective way to reach enlightenment. He recommended giving simple gifts—pure water to drink, food, shelter, clothing, transportation, light, flowers. Even poor people can be generous, he said, by giving a crumb of their food to an ant. Each time we give something away, whether it is a material object or our time (is it "ours"?), we are letting go of a bit of that carefully gathered and fiercely defended temporary heap of stuff we call "I, me, and mine."

FINAL WORDS: Generosity is the highest virtue, and anonymous giving is the highest form of generosity.

10

Just Three Breaths

THE EXERCISE: As many times a day as you are able, give the mind a short rest. For the duration of three breaths ask the inner voices to be silent. It's like turning off the inner radio or TV for a few minutes. Then open all your senses and just be aware—of color, sound, touch, and smell.

Reminding Yourself

Post notes in your environment with the number 3 on them. You could add a drawing of a person with an empty thought balloon above his head. It might help to set an alarm or cell phone to ring at irregular intervals throughout the day.

Discoveries

When people first begin meditating or doing contemplative prayer, they experience a measure of relief from the constantly churning mind. They are happy. If their concentration deepens, however, they are often dismayed to find that their mind is like a hyperactive two-year-old, unable to sit still, at rest in the present moment, for more than a few minutes. It is busy all day long. It journeys to the past, reliving past pleasures and hurts. It darts off into the future, making a hundred plans. It escapes into fantasies, creating imaginary worlds to fulfill all its desires. New meditators also discover their inner voices, which are constantly narrating, comparing and criticizing, rationalizing. At this stage people confess that they are thinking of quitting meditation. Their mind seems noisier than ever! As soon as their mind wanders off the practice, they are filled with self-criticism. Instead of progressing, they seem to be going backward.

It is as if the mind is willing to go along with the game of quieting itself only for a short while. When it realizes that we are quite serious about making it still, and even existing for periods of time without its constant direction, it can panic and begin to spin like a squirrel in a cage. The mind goes into self-protection mode, trying to pinpoint the source of trouble, generating judgment of others and criticism of self. When these negative thoughts and emotions fill the mind, it can undermine and eventually destroy mindfulness practice.

The simple practice of just three breaths can come as a relief. It can interrupt this kind of downward spiral and renew our practice. We ask the mind to rest a bit, to be completely still, just for three breaths. Because we don't have to count three breaths, we can enjoy them. When the three breaths are done, let the mind loose for a bit, then turn its full attention again to just three breaths. As the mind rests more and more in the present moment, it will naturally settle. Then, without effort, we can be present for a few more breaths, and then just a few more, until we are able to sit in relaxed, open awareness.

Deeper Lessons

Even at night our mind does not rest. It creates dreams and processes the undigested material from our days. All this mental activity, all these choices and possibilities, is confusing and even exhausting. Just as the body needs regular rest, so too does the mind.

To rest the mind in complete stillness, in pure awareness, is to return it to its Original Nature, its natural state. This task helps us break the habit of compulsive thinking. We don't need the mind to narrate all the events of our life. We don't need the mind to comment internally on everything and everyone we encounter. This narration, this commentary, separates us from just experiencing life as it is.

The mind has two functions: thinking and awareness. When we are newborn babies, we have no words in our mind. We live in pure awareness. When we learn to speak, words begin to fill our mind and mouth. My two-year-old granddaughter chatters all day long, just to practice her new skill of talking, and she basks in the smiles and praise it brings from adults around her. Learning to talk is a necessary developmental step, but it is also the beginning of a mind that is always speaking inside our heads. This internal talking takes energy. The mind truly rests only when we are able to turn off its thinking function and turn on its awareness function. Usually we wait to do this until we have at least thirty minutes to meditate or center ourselves in prayer. However, we can also sprinkle short moments of mind-rest throughout the day. When our mind does rest, even for a period as short as three breaths, it can become refreshed and clear.

The Buddha talked about the unrestrained mind as a feral elephant. Its strength is dissipated as it runs around wildly. To harness its power, we must first tie it to a stake. This is what we do when we tie the mind to the breath. Then we teach the elephant to stand still. We teach the mind to empty itself and stand ready, alert but relaxed, waiting for whatever will appear next.

When the mind switches from productive to receptive mode, we return to the pure awareness of infancy. We are able to plug back in to the unlimited Source. Afterward the rejuvenated mind asks, "Why don't we do this more often?"

FINAL WORDS: Prescription for health: Quiet the mind for just three breaths. Repeat as needed.

11

Entering New Spaces

THE EXERCISE: Our shorthand for this mindfulness practice is "mindfulness of doors," but it actually involves bringing awareness to any transitions between spaces, when you leave one kind of space and enter another. Before you walk through a door, pause, even for a second, and take one breath. Be aware of the differences you might feel in each new space you enter.

Part of this practice is to pay careful attention to how you close the door when entering a new space. We often move immediately into a new space without finishing up with the old one, forgetting to close the door or letting it slam shut.

Reminding Yourself

Put an obvious sticker, such as a big star, on the doors you commonly encounter at home. Also remember doors to closets, garages, sheds, basements, and offices. Or you can put a special mark such as a letter D on the back of the hand you use to open doors.

Discoveries

Don't be discouraged if at first you don't succeed in carrying out this task. It is one of the most difficult tasks we've undertaken at the monastery over the years. You find yourself walking toward a door, thinking, "Door. Door. Be mindful walking through the . . ." and suddenly you find yourself on the other side of the door, with no awareness of how you passed through it. After doing this task for a week once or twice a year we have become better at it, eventually becoming aware of entering new spaces even when there wasn't a helpful barrier such as a door.

Differences in spaces are most obvious when you step from indoors to outdoors. There are clear changes in temperature, air quality, smell, light, sound, and even feeling tone. With practice we can also detect these kinds of differences, though they are more subtle, when we enter or exit the many different indoor spaces we move through in a day.

One person used a counter to keep track of the number of doors he passed through—over 240 in one day! That's a lot of potential mindfulness moments. This task seems to spawn creativity and also new tasks. For example, one person added the practice of noticing "doors" in her mind closing and opening as she let go of one train of thought and began another. She became most aware of entering new "rooms" in her mind during meditation. Another person, who had a lifelong habit of slamming doors, worked on closing doors gently. Another tried to make her mind as big as the space in each new room she entered.

Deeper Lessons

It took many of us, including me, several weeks of repeating this task until we were able to bring mindfulness to even half of the doors we walked through. We improved when someone hung a large sheet of Plexiglas in a dim hallway near a commonly used door. We all walked into it several times, even the person who hung it up! A few bangs on the head can do wonders for one's mindfulness.

We also pondered why this exercise was so challenging. One person had an insight: as we walk toward a door, our mind moves ahead to the future, toward what we will be encountering and doing on the other side. This mind movement is not obvious. It takes careful watching. It makes us go unconscious, just briefly, of what we are doing in the present. The unconscious or semiconscious mind, however, is able to steer us through the movements of opening the door and making our way safely through.

This is one example of how we move through much of our day like sleepwalkers, navigating through the world while caught in a dream. This semiconscious state is a source of dissatisfaction (*dukkha* in Sanskrit), the persistent feeling that something is not right, that there is a gap between us and life as it is actually happening. As we learn to become present, bit by bit, the gap closes and life becomes more vivid and satisfying.

FINAL WORDS: Appreciate each physical space and each mind space that you encounter.

12

Rest Your Hands

THE EXERCISE: Several times a day let your hands relax completely. For at least a few seconds, let them be completely still. One way to do this is to place them in your lap and then focus your awareness on the subtle sensations in the quiet hands.

Reminding Yourself

Wear your watch backward. If you don't wear a watch, put a string or rubber band around your wrist.

Discoveries

The hands are always busy. If they are not busy, they are somewhat tense, ready to work.

The hands reveal our state of mental ease or discomfort. Many people have unconscious nervous hand gestures, such as rubbing or wringing their hands, touching their face, tapping a finger, snapping a fingernail, cracking their knuckles, or twiddling their thumbs. When people first learn to meditate, they often have a hard time letting the hands be still. They may restlessly rearrange the position of their hands, and as soon as there is a small itch, the hands fly up to scratch it.

When we relax our hands, the rest of the body and even the mind will relax too. Relaxing the hands is a way of quieting the mind. We also found that when the hands are quiet in our lap, we can listen more attentively.

As I did this task, I discovered that my hands tighten on the steering wheel when I am driving. Now I can check for this unconscious habit and relax my grip. I realized that I can hold the wheel with a lighter grip and still drive safely. When I relax my hands on the steering wheel, I often find that ten minutes later, they have resumed their habitual tight grip again. This is why we call it mindfulness "practice." We have to do it over and over again to truly become aware. We set out to do the practice, then revert to unconscious behavior, then become aware again, then start the practice again, and so on.

Body and mind work together. When we put the mind at ease, the body can relax. When the body is still, the mind can settle. The health of both is improved.

Tension is not necessary for most of the tasks of our life. It is a waste of energy. There is a meditation called a "body scan" that can first help us discover unconscious tension lurking in the body and can then help us soften or dispel it. It goes like this: You sit quietly and focus your awareness on one part of the body at a time, beginning at the top. What are the sensations coming from the scalp and hair? Once you are aware of these sensations, try to notice any extra holding or tension you may be doing and try to gently soften or release it as you breathe out. Next move on to the forehead, then the eyes, and so on, one body part at a time. It is interesting to discover how much tension is unconsciously held, and in which body parts.

We generally go through most of our lives in one of two modes. At night we are lying down, relaxed and asleep. When the alarm clock rings, we get up and switch to the mode we use during the day: upright, holding tension, and alert. There are not many times in our busy lives when we are both upright and relaxed. (Unfortunately there are also times when we are lying down and are neither relaxed nor asleep. We are instead brooding, anxious, and restlessly shifting, unable to sleep.)

Being awake, alert, and relaxed is a state we may experience on a vacation day. We wake up later than usual, fully rested, and lie in bed a while without anything on our mind or anything to accomplish. We hear the birds and the garbageman, but there is no tension in the body or mind. My mother used to call this "the time in-between, my best time to ponder important things." This is true; it is the best time, because the mind unclouded by worries about the survival of "I, me, and mine" can look more deeply into important matters. In meditation we purposely widen this in-between state. We purposely become relaxed while remaining upright and alert. It isn't easy at first. We tip over into worry that our meditation isn't perfect, that we won't become enlightened. Our shoulders begin to ache with tension. Or we tip over into drowsiness, relaxed and almost falling over, until a noise surprises us awake. It takes us a while to get our balance.

FINAL WORDS: Remember to relax the hands, and with them, the whole body and mind.

13

Say Yes

THE EXERCISE: In this practice we say yes to everyone and everything that happens. When you notice the impulse to disagree, consider whether it is really necessary. Could you just nod, or even be silent but pleasant? Whenever it is not dangerous to you or others, agree with others and with what is happening in your life.

Reminding Yourself

Put stickers with the word "Yes" in spots where you'll notice them in your home and workplace. Write "Yes" on the back of your hand so you see it frequently.

Discoveries

This task helps us see how often we take a stance that is negative or oppositional. If we are able to watch our mind when someone is talking to us, particularly if they are asking us to do something, we can see our thoughts forming defenses and counterarguments. Can we resist the desire to disagree verbally when the issue is not critical? Can we watch our mental and physical attitude to things that arise in a typical day? Is our automatic thought "Oh no"?

Our habitual oppositional stance can take the form of thoughts ("I don't agree with what he's saying"), body language (tensing muscles, arms crossed), speech ("That's a stupid idea"), or action (shaking the head, rolling the eyes, ignoring someone who's talking).

People in certain professions report that they have difficulty with this task. Lawyers, for example, are trained to detect flaws in a contract or faults in what a witness or another lawyer is saying. Academics are trained to criticize one another's theories and research. Success at work may depend on "attack mind," but when you spend an entire day cultivating this attitude, it can be difficult to turn it off when you arrive home.

While doing this task, one person

noted that an external "yes" might not match the real attitude of "no" inside, and that the task helped him detect a hidden constricted state of mind. Another man found that he usually responds to requests by weighing other considerations—namely, all the other things he has to do. He found it freeing to just say yes and thus let go of all the internal effort involved in making a decision. It felt generous. Another person said that saying yes created the experience of ease, of going with the flow of people who came into her office rather than resisting it. This task may be modified according to circumstances. You can hold an inward "yes" to your child's wish to jump on furniture but redirect their energy to the playground instead.

Deeper Lessons

The Buddhist tradition describes three poisons of the mind: greed, aversion, and ignorance. We developed this task for Zen students who seem particularly afflicted by aversion, those who habitually resist anything asked of them and what comes forward in life. Their initial and unconscious response to anything asked of them is "no," expressed either in body language or out loud. Sometimes the no is expressed as "yes, but . . . ," and sometimes it is cloaked in reasonable language, but it is still a consistent and persistent pattern of opposition.

People who are stuck in aversion often make major life decisions based not on moving toward a positive goal but rather on moving away from something they perceive to be negative. They are reactive rather than proactive: "My parents didn't pay their bills on time and our electricity got turned off; I'm going to become an accountant," instead of "I want to become an accountant because I love numbers."

When monks enter training at Japanese Soto Zen monasteries, they are told that the only acceptable response to anything they are asked to do in the first year of training is "Hai! (Yes!)." This is powerful training. It cuts through layers of apparent maturity, down to the defiant two-year-old and/or teenager within.

Not expressing opposition helps us let go of self-centered views and see that our personal opinion is actually not so important after all. It's surprising how often our disagreement with another person is actually unimportant and only serves to increase our distress and the suffering of those around us. Saying yes can be energizing, since habitual resistance is a persistent drain on our life energy.

FINAL WORDS: Cultivate an internal attitude of "yes" to life and all it brings you. It will save you lots of energy.

14

Bottoms of the Feet

THE EXERCISE: As often as possible during the day, place your awareness in the bottoms of your feet. Become aware of the sensations on the bottoms of the feet such as the pressure of the floor or ground beneath the feet, or the warmth or coolness of the feet. It is particularly important to do so whenever you notice yourself becoming anxious or upset.

Reminding Yourself

The classic method for remembering this task is to put a small stone in your shoe. A less painful, though probably less effective, way is to place notes that say "Feet" where you'll see them, or cutouts of footprints in appropriate locations on the floor. You could also set your cell phone or timer to ring at certain intervals during the day, and whenever you hear the ringer, turn your awareness to the bottoms of your feet.

Discoveries

Through this mindfulness practice, people noticed that ordinarily they walked about without paying much attention to their feet, unless their feet were hurting or they stumbled. If people were caught up in thinking, moving their awareness from the head to the feet had the effect of settling the mind. This probably occurs because the bottoms of the feet are as far as we can get from the head, where we often seem to think our "selves" are located. We identify very closely with our thoughts and give our mind/brain an exalted status. Many of us unconsciously view the body merely as a servant of the brain—the body is equipped with feet to transport the commanding mind around, and with hands to get things the mind thinks it wants, such as doughnuts.

We often begin meals at the monastery by sitting in silence and placing our awareness in the bottoms of our feet. It helps us bring mindfulness to eating. We've also found that when we are aware of the bottoms of the feet, our balance improves and we are more sure-footed.

Martial arts and yoga emphasize being aware of the feet and mentally extending a sense of connection or roots down into the earth. This gives rise to both physical stability and mental equanimity. When we become anxious, the mind becomes more active, like a hamster in an exercise wheel, spinning around, trying to figure out how to escape mental or physical discomfort. Doing this task, people discover that when they bring awareness to all the tiny sensations on the bottoms of the feet, the flow of ever-changing physical sensations fills the mind completely and there is no room at all for thinking. They feel less top-heavy, more anchored, less likely to be pushed about by thoughts and emotions. Dropping awareness into the bottoms of the feet clears the mind and lifts clouds of anxiety.

Deeper Lessons

Our mind likes to think. It thinks that if it is not thinking, it is failing at its job of guiding and protecting us. However, when the mind becomes overactive, the opposite occurs. Its guidance becomes shrill, even cruel, and its constant warnings fill us with anxiety. How can we put the thinking mind in its proper place and perspective? We shift the mind from thinking to awareness, beginning with full awareness of the body.

An essential aspect of Zen practice is walking meditation, called *kinhin*. We do it without shoes so that the sensations on the bottoms of the feet will be maximized. Walking meditation helps bring the quiet body/mind of seated meditation into our ordinary active world. Silent walking is a bridge between one side of meditation—silent sitting in pure awareness—and the other side—speaking and moving about. It is not so easy to keep the mind still while walking. Any movement of the body seems to produce movement of the mind.

We can challenge ourselves. Can I keep my mind still and focused in the bottoms of my feet for one or two circuits around the room? Or for the entire length of an outdoor walking path? Or from here to the corner?

FINAL WORDS: Placing your awareness in the bottoms of your feet will lead to mental stability and emotional serenity, if you practice it diligently.

15

One Bite at a Time

THE EXERCISE: This is a mindfulness practice to do whenever you are eating. After you take a bite, put the spoon or fork back down in the bowl or on the plate. Place your awareness in your mouth until that one bite has been enjoyed and swallowed. Only then pick up the utensil and take another bite. If you are eating with your hands, put the sandwich, apple, or cookie down between bites.

Reminding Yourself

Post notes with "One Bite at a Time" wherever you eat, or an icon of a spoon or fork with the words "Put It Down!"

Discoveries

This is one of the most challenging mindful-eating practices we do at our monastery. In attempting this exercise, most people discover that they have the habit of "layering" bites of food. That is, they put one bite in the mouth, divert their attention away from the mouth as they shovel food onto the fork or spoon for the next bite, then put a second bite in the mouth before the first one is swallowed. Often the hand is hovering in the air, with another bite halfway to the mouth, as the preceding bite is chewed. They discover that as soon as the mind wanders, the hand assumes control again, putting new bites of food in on top of partially processed bites. It is amazing how hard this simple task can be. It takes time, patience, persistence, and a sense of humor to change long-term habits.

The absorption of food can begin in the mouth, if we chew our food well and let it mix with saliva, which contains digestive enzymes. The earlier absorption begins, the earlier the satiation signals are sent out to the brain, and the sooner we feel full. The sooner we feel full, the more appropriate we can be about the amounts of food we serve ourselves and then consume.

Putting down your utensil between bites used to be part of good manners. It counteracts the tendency to wolf down our food. One person exclaimed after trying this task, "I just realized that I never chew my food. I swallow it almost whole, in my haste to get the next bite in!" She had to ask herself, "Why am I in such a rush to get through a meal, when I enjoy eating so much?"

Deeper Lessons

This is actually a task about becoming aware of impatience. Eating quickly, layering one bite on top of another, is a specific example of impatience. Doing this task may lead you to watch the arising of impatience in other aspects and occasions in your life. Do you get impatient when you have to wait? We have to ask ourselves, "Why am I in such a rush to get through life, when I want to enjoy it so much?"

Experiencing one bite or one swallow at a time is a way of experiencing one moment at a time. Since we eat or drink at least three times a day, this mindfulness tool gives us several built-in opportunities to bring mindfulness into each day. Eating is naturally pleasurable, but when we eat quickly and without mindfulness, we don't experience that pleasure. Research shows that, ironically, people eat their favorite foods more quickly than foods they dislike! Binge eaters also report that they keep on eating in an effort to re-create the pleasure of the first bite. Because the taste receptors tire quickly, this can never work.

When the mind is absent, thinking about the past or future, we are only half tasting our food. When our awareness rests in the mouth, when we are fully present as we eat, when we slow our eating down, pausing between bites, then each bite can be like the first, rich and full of interesting sensations.

Pursuing pleasure without mindfulness is like being caught on a treadmill. Mindfulness allows pleasure to bloom in thousands of small moments in our life.

FINAL WORDS: There can be no party in the mouth if the mind is not invited to attend.

16

Study Suffering

THE EXERCISE: As you go about your day, pay attention to the phenomenon of suffering. How do you detect it in yourself or in others? Where is it most obvious? What are the milder forms? What are the more intense forms?

Reminding Yourself

Post notes that say "Study Suffering," or photos of an unhappy person, in appropriate places.

Discoveries

Suffering is everywhere. We see it in people's anxious faces, hear it in their voices, see it on the news. As we study suffering, we can hear it in our own thoughts, feel it in our own bodies, see it in the face in the mirror. Often people begin this exercise thinking of suffering in its extreme and obvious forms: the death of someone you love, or children who are victims of war. As this task brings increased awareness, people discover that there is a spectrum of suffering, from mild irritation and impatience to rage or overwhelming grief.

We are exposed to the suffering not just of people but of animals as well. We see the suffering of those we love and also the suffering of strangers on the street. Suffering pours into our hearts and minds through the radio, TV, and Internet.

There is a difference between pain and suffering. Pain is the unpleasant physical sensations experienced by all human bodies, indeed all sentient beings. Suffering is the mental and emotional distress that is added to these physical sensations. The Buddha studied suffering meticulously for seven years and discovered that physical pain is inevitable, but the suffering added by the mind is optional. Actually, it is optional only if you have good tools to work with the mind and if you apply them diligently.

For example, when we have a headache, we can think, "OK, I have temporary discomfort in this area of the body." Or we can think:

"This is the second headache I've had this week." [Dragging the past into the present.]

"I'm sure it's going to get worse, like it did before." [Predicting and perhaps creating future events.]

"I can't stand it." [But, in actuality, you have before and you will again.]

"What's wrong with me?" [Nothing. You are a human being with a body.]

"Could I have a brain tumor?" [Extremely unlikely, but you can give yourself a much worse headache worrying about it.]

"Maybe it's the stress I'm under at work. My boss is impossible. . . ." [Casting around for someone to blame.]

Does our mental distress help cure the physical pain? No, it only makes it stronger and prolongs it. We have taken simple temporary physical discomfort and turned it into a mass of suffering.

Deeper Lessons

There are some benefits to suffering. If we never experienced suffering, we would coast along in life with no motivation to change. Unfortunately it seems to be true that we are the most motivated to change when we are the most unhappy.

If we can restrain the mind from running amok, speculating and disaster-mongering, looking for someone to blame for our misery, then we can just experience the physical aspects of what we call "pain." If we just experience it, actually investigate it, discerning all its qualities, instead of it being "unbearable," it can become quite interesting. What size is the focus of pain? Exactly where is it located—above or below the skull? What is its texture—sharp, dull, prickly, or smooth? If it had a color, what would it be? Is it constant or intermittent? People often report interesting discoveries when they stop resisting pain and investigate it in this way. Resistance locks pain in. When we are not adding mental and emotional stress to simple physical discomfort, the pain is free to change and even to dissolve.

Suffering also gives birth to compassion in our hearts. After my first child was born, a new awareness of the fragility of life was also born, and I cried for all the unknown women around the world whose children had died. When we are in pain or distress, it is a perfect time to change the direction of our awareness from inward to outward and to do loving-kindness practice for all who suffer the same way that we are suffering right now. For example, when we are sick with the flu, we could say, "May all those who are sick in bed today, including me, be at ease. May we all rest well and recover quickly."

In the same way that being sick helps us appreciate good health, as we become aware of many kinds of suffering, we also become more aware of its opposite, the many simple sources of happiness—the perfect eyelashes of a baby, the smell of the first drops of rain on a dusty road, the slanting shafts of sunlight in a quiet room.

FINAL WORDS: Suffering gives us the motivation to change. Whether that change is positive or negative is up to us. Suffering also gives us the gift of empathy for all who suffer as we do.

17

Notice Smells

THE EXERCISE: During this week, as often as possible, become aware of smells and fragrance. This may be easiest to do when you are eating or drinking, but try it at other times too. Several times a day, try sniffing the air like a dog. If there are not many smells in your environment, you might try creating some smells that you can detect. You could dab some vanilla on your wrist, or boil some spices, such as cinnamon or cloves, in water on the stove.

You could also try lighting a few scented candles or sniffing scented oils.

Reminding Yourself

Post the word "Smell" or an image of a nose in helpful places.

Discoveries

The cells that respond to smells in the back of our nose are just two synapses away from the processing centers in our primitive brain for emotion and memories, so odors can evoke powerful conditioned responses: desire or aversion. These unconscious responses can occur even when we are not aware of detecting an odor. We don't appreciate our sense of smell until we lose it—for example, when we have a cold. People who lose their sense of smell permanently can become depressed, since they also lose their previous enjoyment of food. Many become anxious that they will not smell smoke from a fire, will fail to detect their own body odor, or will eat spoiled food.

When practicing mindfulness of smell people discover that there are many smells in their environment, some obvious (coffee, cinnamon rolls, gasoline, skunk) and many that are more subtle (fresh air as we step outside, soap or shaving cream on our own face, clean sheets). They also discover that smell can evoke emotions such as desire or aversion.

The rich experience of what we call flavor is mostly due to our sense of smell. Our tongue is able to register only a few sensations—salty, sweet, sour, bitter, and umami (savory, such as in meat or soy sauce)—but we can distinguish several thousand odors and as little as one molecule of some substances. Research shows that women have more sensitive noses than men. Women may wear perfume to attract men, but the effort is probably wasted. The fragrances men pick as favorites are the smell of baking bread, vanilla, and grilling meat.

In reality, there are no "good" or "bad" smells. We become accustomed to common smells around us. When I lived in Africa, people around me had a strong aroma of sweat mixed with wood smoke. It was undoubtedly a comforting smell to a child who had been surrounded by that fragrance since birth. Probably I smelled funny to them, and they could also detect me coming in the dark. When East and West first met,

Japanese people, who bathed daily, disliked the smell of Europeans, who ate dairy products and took baths infrequently. They called the visitors "stinks of butter." One is not very aware of the odor of one's own body. Other people may tell us, to our surprise, that we need to take a shower or that we have a delicious smell. Just as we are not aware of the scent of our own body, we are not aware of the "scent" of our own personality. How does that affect others?

Deeper Lessons

Much of our behavior is directed by unconscious conditioning. We meet a person who looks, dresses, speaks, or even smells like someone who wounded us in our childhood, and we feel an instant, inexplicable aversion toward this innocent person. It has nothing to do with them. It is just an electrical phenomenon, sense impressions causing neurons to fire and connect to storage sites in the brain for old memories and emotions. To transform these habitual patterns is not easy. First we have to bring the light of awareness to the body sensations, thoughts, and emotions as they arise. We have to watch carefully the junction between sensation and feeling tone, which is the seed crystal that will start a chain reaction that ends in thought, emotion, speech, and behavior (or what Buddhists call karma).

The cascade of sensation → feeling tone → perception → action happens so fast that it is hard to see the individual steps. But people can understand this chain of events when it involves smell. Let's say you step outside and take a deep breath. You detect a smell and recoil internally. Why? As chemical molecules hit the inside of your nose, you smelled something, and it caused a negative feeling tone, before your mind knew what it was. Then your mind tried to identify it—"Oh, dog feces." This is perception, which is then followed by volitional action. You might say, "What idiot let their dog poop on my lawn?!" Or you might just walk inside to get a plastic bag to clean it up.

Odor can have a powerful effect on our mental-emotional state and behavior. Smells can call up memories and old reactions. For example, the smell of a certain aftershave your father used could make you either happy and affectionate or irritable and standoffish, depending on how you and your dad got along. Psychologists sometimes use disgusting smells to decondition destructive impulses or behaviors, such as addiction to pornography.

Positive conditioning to smell can be helpful. One reason incense is used in meditation halls is that over time a strong link is forged between the fragrance of incense and a quiet, concentrated state of mind. As you enter the scented hall, your mind automatically settles. Monks become so sensitive to smell during long hours of meditation that they can tell when the meditation period is over by the smell of the incense. It changes when the burning tip reaches the bed of ash in the incense bowl.

We can be very alert to fragrance when our mind is quiet and input to the other senses is minimal. One night I was sitting outdoors at a temple in Japan, in the deep dark of the monastery's forest of giant bamboo. It was the seventh day of a silent retreat. The air was fresh after two days of typhoon rain. My mind was completely still and my awareness open wide. In the silence I could hear a single bamboo leaf softly falling, down, down. Gradually I became aware of a subtle spicy fragrance. It came from the bamboo. I have never been able to smell it since. I will always remember its delicate perfume, and that remembering evokes in me the sublime peace of that night.

FINAL WORDS: One of the most subtly pleasurable meditations is to be fully aware of smell, how it changes with each in-breath and out-breath.

18

This Person Could Die Tonight

THE EXERCISE: Several times a day, when someone is talking to you, in person or on the telephone, remind yourself, "This person could die tonight. This may be the last time I will be with them." Notice any changes in how you listen, speak, or interact with them.

Reminding Yourself

Put a note on your bathroom mirror, just above or below where your own reflection appears, saying, "This Person Could Die Tonight." Put similar notes near your telephone or in your workspace—places where you're likely to see them while you're interacting with others.

Discoveries

Some people find this exercise a bit depressing at first, but they soon discover that when they become aware of their own mortality and that of the person they are talking to, they listen and pay attention in a different way. Their heart opens as they hold the truth that this could be the very last time they will see this person alive. When we talk to people, especially people we see daily, we are easily distracted and only half listen. We often look a bit to the side or down at something else, rather than directly at them. We might even be annoyed that they have interrupted us. It takes the realization that they could die to make us look at them anew.

This practice becomes particularly poignant when the person you are talking to is aged or ill, or when death has recently taken an acquaintance or someone you loved. When the Japanese say good-bye to someone, they stand respectfully, watching and waving until the car or train is out of sight. This custom has its origin in the awareness that this could be the last time they will see one another. How sad we would feel if our last encounter with our child, partner, or parent were flavored with impatience or anger! How comforting if we had said good-bye with care.

Deeper Lessons

Although sickness, old age, and death come to everyone who has been born into this world, we carry out our lives as if this will not be true for us or those we care about. This practice helps us break through our denial that human life is quite fragile and that death could come at any moment. All it takes is a slight change in the potassium level in our blood, a virulent bacteria, an oncoming driver who falls asleep, or an odd electrical pattern in our heart. Occasionally the veil of denial lifts and we see the truth of the fragility of human life, such as when a coworker or a family member is diagnosed with a fatal illness or when someone our age or younger dies unexpectedly.

Of course we do not want to fill our mind with constant, anxious thoughts about mortality, but an awareness of impermanence can help us cherish the people we encounter every day. When the veil is parted, and we experience the truth that every human life is brief, our conversations change. Instead of talking "to" someone, with a mind half full of other thoughts, we bring more presence to each encounter. This quiet attentiveness is an unusual occurrence in the world of ordinary human beings.

We fall asleep each night in complete trust that we will awaken. When we realize that we too could die tonight, we can become more present, more alive within each moment of our life.

At our Zen monastery, we have a

chant that is sung at the end of each day of a silent retreat. You may wish to recite it each night for a week before you go to sleep:

May I respectfully remind you,
Life and death are of supreme importance.
Time swiftly passes by and opportunity is lost.
When this day has passed, our days of life will be decreased by one.
Each of us should strive to awaken.
Awaken!
Take heed!
Do not squander your life!

FINAL WORDS: Becoming aware of death opens our awareness to this single, vivid moment of life.

19

Hot and Cold

THE EXERCISE: Pay attention during this week to the sensations of heat and cold. Notice any physical or emotional reaction to temperature or temperature changes. Practice being at ease no matter what the temperature is.

Reminding Yourself

You can put up little signs with an image of a thermometer, or with the words "Hot and Cold."

Discoveries

Doing this exercise, we watch our aversion to temperatures outside of a small range. Each person's range is different. We complain, "It's too hot!" or "It's too cold!" as if it shouldn't be that way—the sun, clouds, and air have conspired to make us uncomfortable. We're always doing something to adjust the temperature—turning heaters and air conditioners on and off, opening and closing windows and doors, donning and shedding clothing. We're never satisfied for long. When the temperature rises above 90 degrees, we long for cooler weather; during cold, rainy winters, we long for sun.

I can remember childhood summers in Missouri. The vinyl upholstery in the car scalded our legs as we got in, and there were pools of sweat under us as we got out. We played outside, got sticky, sweaty, and never complained. It was just the way it was. Parents of young children often remark that when they go to the beach, their kids will get in the water and have a ball no matter what the temperature of the ocean. What happens as we mature that makes us intolerant of the way things are?

Once, we were on peace pilgrimage in Japan in August, where stepping out the door felt like we were entering a sauna. Within a few minutes our clothes were soaked through with sweat. After a few hours salt encrusted our skin and made white rings on our clothes. It was so hard not to give vent to our discomfort. But we noticed that the Japanese people, from babies to very old people, were just going about their business, apparently unaffected. It inspired us to let go of complaining-mind and just be present with things as they were, sensations as merely sensations, the wet and dry places, the hot exterior and cool interior, the tickling of trickling sweat. The suffering inflicted by the mind lifted and we became much happier pilgrims.

A woman came to me during a retreat saying that despite extra layers of clothing and a hot-water bottle, she felt cold all the time. She also realized that she was frightened about feeling cold. She knew the fear was irrational, and she had been looking for its source. Then she remembered an incident twenty years earlier when she'd had some heart trouble and was very cold.

I asked her to scan her body carefully and tell me what percentage of the body did not feel cold. After a few minutes she reported with surprise that over 90 percent of her body felt warm, or even hot. She realized that the 10 percent of her body that was cool was producing 100 percent of the fear. Later she said that a weight had been lifted from her mind, a fear that had lasted decades, and she was now able to easily tolerate different temperatures.

I once watched a passenger get into my car and reach over to turn on the air conditioner, before the car had even started. It's like salting our food before we taste it. We live on automatic, trying to insulate ourselves against any discomfort before it even arrives. Then we lose the joy of potential discovery and the freedom of finding that we can investigate, and even be happy, within a greater range of experiences than we thought.

Deeper Lessons

A very important way to work with discomfort is to stop avoiding it. You walk right into it and feel from within the body what is true. You investigate the discomfort—its size, shape, surface texture, and even its color or sound. Is it constant or intermittent? When you are this attentive, when your meditative absorption is deep, what we call discomfort or pain begins to shift and even disappear. It becomes a series of sensations just appearing and disappearing in empty space, twinkling on and off. It is most interesting.

In Japan the *zendo,* or meditation hall, is not heated in winter. The windows are open. It is just like sitting outside except that you don't get rained or snowed on—much. During one February-long retreat

I put on every bit of clothing in my suitcase, so many layers I could barely bend my knees to sit. My skin was so icy it was painful to let my attention rest on my exposed face or hands even briefly. During traditional Zen retreats you eat your meals in the zendo. While eating I had to look to see if the chopsticks were still wedged in my numb fingers. There was no way out of this discomfort. The only way to go was in, placing an unwavering concentration deep in my belly, in the *hara,* or center of the body. It was a powerful retreat, and I understood why the revered Zen master Sogaku Harada Roshi insisted that his monastery be built deep in the snow country.

We spend so much effort trying to make external conditions suit us. However, it is impossible for us to remain comfortable all the time, for the nature of all things is change. This attempt at control is at the heart of our physical exhaustion and emotional distress. There is a Zen koan about this. A monk asked Master Tozan, "Cold and heat descend upon us. How can we avoid them?" Tozan replied, "Why don't you go to the place where there is no cold or heat?" The monk was puzzled and asked, "Where is the place where there is no cold or heat?" Tozan said, "When it is cold, let it be so cold that it kills you. When hot, let it be so hot that it kills you."

In this teaching, "kill you" means kill your ideas about how things have to be for you to be happy. It may sound odd, but you can be practicing mindfulness with discomfort or pain and be quite happy. This happiness comes from the pleasure of just being present, and also from the confidence that you are gaining—confidence that, with ongoing practice, you will eventually be able to face whatever life brings you, even pain, aided by tools such as mindfulness.

FINAL WORDS: When your mind says "too hot" or "too cold," don't believe it. Investigate the entire body's experience of heat and cold.

20

Notice Dislike

THE EXERCISE: Become aware of aversion, the arising of negative feelings toward something or someone. These could be mild feelings, such as irritation, or strong feelings, such as anger and hatred. Try to see what happened just before the aversion arose. What sense impressions occurred—sight, sound, touch, taste, smell, or thought? When does aversion first arise during the day?

Reminding Yourself

Post the words "Notice Dislike" in places where aversion might arise, such as on your mirror, TV, computer monitor, and car dashboard. You could also use small pictures of someone frowning.

Discoveries

When we do this exercise, we find that aversion is more common in our mental/emotional landscape than we realized. It may begin our day, arising when the alarm rings, or as we get out of bed and find that our back hurts. It can be triggered by events on the morning news, by a long line at the subway or gas station, or by an encounter with family, coworkers, or clients.

Once I was waiting in the car for my husband to come out of the house. I looked idly out the window and noticed that near the fence many long dandelions had grown up and were going to seed. Instantaneously an impulse arose to jump out of the car, grab some pruning shears, and whack them back into submission. This was accompanied by the thought "Off with their heads!" I realized that this was the seed of anger, the seed of all the wars waged on this earth, lying dormant within me. It's not that I hate dandelions. Their bright golden faces are a wonderful thing to meditate upon. Close up, they can change a negative mind-state quite quickly. It's not that I intend to let them flourish, but if I trim that part of the lawn, I will wait until I am not doing it from aversion. I might ride the mower practicing appreciation for the life of the dandelions and loving-kindness for all the beings who make their home in the grass and weeds.

Deeper Lessons

It may be dismaying to discover how pervasive aversion is in even a single day in a life that we might describe as happy. It is, however, very important to become aware that feelings of dislike are ubiquitous in our daily lives. Aversion is one of the three afflictive mind-states described in the Buddhist tradition: greed (or clinging), aversion (or pushing away), and delusion (or ignoring). They are called afflictive because they afflict us the way a virus afflicts us, causing distress and pain not only to ourselves but to those around us.

Aversion is the hidden source of anger and aggression. It arises from the notion that if we could just manage to get rid of something or someone, then we would be happy. What we humans wish to get rid of in order to become happy could be as trivial as a mosquito or as large as a nation.

There are few ideas more absurd than the notion, "If I could arrange things—and people—to be just as I want them, then I would be happy." It is absurd for at least two reasons. First of all, even if we had the power to make everything in the world perfect for us, that perfection could last for only a second because all the other people in the world have different ideas of how they would like things to be and are working to get them their way. Our "perfect" is not perfect to anyone else. Secondly, forcing perfection on the world is bound to fail because of the truth of impermanence—nothing lasts forever.

Sometimes as I am walking around the monastery, I notice a subtle flavor in my mind. It is a faint but pervasive sense of aversion. It comes from what I consider to be part of my job: noticing things that need to be fixed or changed. It comes from noticing imperfection. When this necessary noticing makes my mind-state go sour, I have to switch for a while to "appreciating things as they are."

Mindfulness practice helps us become at ease no matter what conditions exist, and no matter how they change. It asks us to see the perfection in all creation. It asks us to become aware of aversion and counteract it with appreciation and loving-kindness.

FINAL WORDS: One of the Buddha's famous sayings is "Anger does not cease through anger, but through love alone." Become aware of aversion within and use the antidote—practice loving-kindness.

21

Listen like a Sponge

THE EXERCISE: Listen to other people as if you were a sponge, soaking up whatever the other person says. Let the mind be quiet, and just take it in. Don't formulate any response in the mind until a response is requested or obviously needed.

Reminding Yourself

Post the words "Listen like a Sponge," or a picture of an ear and a sponge, in relevant places.

Discoveries

At our monastery we call this practice absorptive listening, and we've discovered that it does not come naturally to most people. Musicians, for example, have been trained to listen with absorptive attention to musical sounds, but that does not mean they are able to listen in the same way when a person is talking to them. Good psychotherapists, on the other hand, use absorptive listening with people all the time. They are attuned to the subtle changes in tone or quality of voice that indicate something deeper than the words, even belying the words—a sticking place, hidden tears or anger—that needs to be explored.

Lawyers are trained to do the opposite, especially if they work in the adversarial atmosphere of the courtroom.

They are listening for the flaws or discrepancies in what someone is saying, while simultaneously forming a rebuttal in their minds. This may work in the courtroom, but it does not go over well at home, with one's spouse or children, in particular with teenage offspring.

When practicing absorptive listening, even people who are not lawyers may notice the presence of an inner attorney—a mental voice saying, "Hurry up and finish talking so I can tell you what I think"—which interferes with tranquil, attentive listening.

People also discover how many times, even in a single minute, they "check out" while someone else is talking. There's a flick of the mind to a shopping list or a future appointment, or a flick of the eyes to notice someone passing by. Absorptive listening is not easy. It is a skill that takes time to learn.

Deeper Lessons

To do absorptive listening, we have to make the body and mind still. This is mindfulness in action, holding a core of stillness within, in a moving, noisy world. When you are listening carefully, you will be aware of your own thoughts as part of the landscape of sound. Like the sound of a passing car, you acknowledge your passing thoughts but are not disturbed by them.

If you are trying this practice with the support of a group or community, one of the most interesting aspects of this exercise is to be on the receiving end—noticing how you feel or react when someone is absorptively listening to *you.*

Most people feel gratitude for being so well witnessed. They feel cherished.

There is a scene that has always touched me in the movie *Shall We Dance?* A man whose marriage has ended asks, "Why do people get married?" His companion says, "Because we need a witness to our lives. You're saying, 'Your life will not go unnoticed because I will witness it.'"

There is a Buddhist recitation for invoking compassion, and it highlights the role of listening in caring for others. "We shall practice listening so attentively that we are able to hear what the other is saying—and also what is left unsaid. We know that by listening deeply we already alleviate a great deal of pain and suffering in the other."

Therapists trained in absorptive listening say that it can, by itself, catalyze healing. There are types of therapy in which the therapist does not say anything, letting the wisdom emerge from clients as they listen to themselves talk.

One student who had been raised in a home where no one ever listened to him said that having someone listen to him with full attention felt like receiving "life-giving manna." Some people find it uncomfortable at first, as it is outside of their life experience to have someone *just* listen to what they are saying. They feel at first as if they are under scrutiny, like a biological specimen.

Absorptive listening can also give you equanimity with the difficult voices in your own mind. When the Inner Critic says something absurd like, "Look at your wrinkles. I hate them!

You shouldn't get old!" you can just be aware of what it says, neither believing it nor reacting.

FINAL WORDS: Absorptive listening is by itself therapeutic, and you don't need a degree in psychology to practice it.

22

Appreciation

THE EXERCISE: Stop throughout the day and consciously identify what you are able to appreciate in this moment. It could be something about yourself, another person, your environment, or what your body is doing or sensing. This is an investigation. Be curious, asking yourself, "Is there anything I can appreciate right now?"

Reminding Yourself

Post in appropriate places the word "Appreciate."

Discoveries

Many people have tried using affirmations to make themselves happier or more positive in outlook, repeating phrases to themselves such as "I am worthy of love," or "Today will be a good day and bring me what I want." Affirmations may be valuable at certain times, but they can also paper over a troubled mind-state. This mindfulness exercise is different.

Appreciation practice is an investigation. Can we find anything, anywhere, in this moment, that is cause for appreciation? We look, listen, feel. Anything? When we take a little time, we may find that there are many things to appreciate, from being dry, clothed, and well fed, to encountering a kind store clerk or the warmth of a cup of tea or coffee in our hand.

One category of things to appreciate is that which we experience as positive, such as having food in our belly. Another category of things to appreciate is the things that are absent, such as illness or war. We don't appreciate their absence until we've suffered their presence. When we recover from a bad flu, for a short while we are glad to be healthy again, grateful not to be vomiting or coughing, happy just to be able to eat and to walk. We don't appreciate health until we've been ill, water until we're thirsty, or electricity until it goes off.

This practice helps us stop, open our senses, and become receptive to what is available in our lives just now.

Deeper Lessons

This practice helps us cultivate joy. The Buddhist term for joy is *mudita*. It means more than just appreciating what makes us feel good. It includes the happiness we feel in connection with other people's joy and good fortune. This quality of joy is not hard to feel when the other people are those we love. For example, we can easily share our child's happiness with a new toy. What happens, however, when someone we dislike or are jealous of is given something we want for ourselves, such as public acclaim or an award? Can we feel joy in their joy? This is not so easy.

Have you ever noticed how the mind focuses on what is wrong—wrong with us, with people around us, with our work, and with the world? Our mind is like a lawyer reading the contract for "my life," always looking for flaws or contract violations. The mind is magnetically drawn to the negative. Just look at the news. What holds readers' or viewers' attention is natural or man-made disasters, wars, fires, shootings, bombings, recall of potentially dangerous toys or cars, epidemics, and scandal. Why is our mind attracted to the negative? It's because the mind doesn't have to be worried about the positive things that might happen. If good things come to pass, well, that's wonderful, but the mind quickly puts these aside. The mind's concern is protecting us from the negative, the dangerous.

Unfortunately this means that negativity begins to color our awareness, often without our even knowing it. If we aren't aware of this subtle downbeat bent of our mind, it can grow unnoticed, leading to dark states of mind such as fear and depression. To counteract this tendency, to turn away from the mental habit of subtle negativity, to become more content with the life we are living, we need the antidote of mudita.

FINAL WORDS: Maezumi Roshi always admonished us, "Appreciate your life!" (He meant both our everyday life and our One Great Life. They are not separate.)

23

Mindful Driving

THE EXERCISE: Bring mindful attention to driving. Notice all the body movements, car movements, sounds, habit patterns, and thoughts involved in driving. (If you do not drive a car, you can bring attention to riding a bike or being a passenger in a car, bus, or train.)

Reminding Yourself

Place a note on your steering wheel or dashboard. It's best to remove the note before you start driving, so as not to create a visual distraction, and to replace the note before you get out of the car so that it will be there to remind you the next time you drive.

Discoveries

People find that this exercise opens up beginner's mind, helping them to step back from driving on autopilot and supporting them in noticing all the subtle movements of driving. We can start this mindfulness exercise right after we get into the car. Feel the pressure of the seat on your thighs, buttocks, and back. Feel your feet resting on the floor. Feel the pressure of the metal key as you turn on the ignition. Feel the vibrations that tell you that the car is running and hasn't stalled. Notice how the hands grip the steering wheel: Top, sides, bottom rim? One hand or two? What emotions arise while driving? For example, people commonly report that when they are cut off by other drivers, they experience bursts of anger that destroy their mental serenity.

I like to pay attention to the feeling of the road, extending my awareness down through the tires into the pavement, as if the car body is my body and the tires are my feet. I pay attention to the bumps and vibrations as the car moves from driveway to street, street to highway. I listen to the sounds of driving—the engine sound, the wind sounds, the tire sounds.

I once drove the Japanese Zen master Harada Roshi from Washington to Oregon. As we crossed the state line, he seemed half asleep, but he immediately remarked on the change in road texture and sound. I was impressed by his continuous level of awareness and vowed to further develop my own.

When we practice mindful driving, we notice that each person has an individual style of driving. Some people drive slowly and timidly, making their passengers impatient, while others accelerate through yellow lights and make their passengers sick on sharp turns. Some drivers look at scenery, eat, and make phone calls while driving; others keep their eyes locked on the road, ready for any contingency.

Mindful driving calls for relaxed, alert awareness. When practicing mindful driving, I envision moving forward in what we call in Zen "one straight line." This means that no matter how many curves there are, no matter how many times you have to come to a complete stop and start up again, no matter how many detours you have to negotiate, you remain aware of your destination and steady in your purpose.

Deeper Lessons

Because modern people spend so much time in vehicles, this exercise helps answer the question "When can I find time to practice mindfulness?" Being mindful in a vehicle can provide many minutes of extra practice each day and help us arrive at our destination feeling refreshed. Like all mindfulness practices, mindful driving includes body, mind, and heart.

The fundamental question underlying all these mindfulness tasks is this: "Are you willing to change?" Mindful driving involves being willing to change our driving habits. Normally we are willing to change only when life isn't working for us, if we are suffering. For example, we might become willing to drive no faster than the speed limit once we get an expensive speeding ticket. Mindfulness practice asks us to change ourselves for a different reason—out of curiosity, because change could lead us to greater freedom and happiness.

I was in a car as a passenger once while a Zen student of mine drove, and I commented on his inattentive driving habits. He immediately asked me, "Please tell me what you see and how I can change." I did and he did. Now he is a very good driver. This is the mind of a true student—to take anything that comes along as an opportunity to change in a way that benefits others.

If you want to experience more peace and contentment, you must examine all aspects of your life, become aware of what kinds of habit patterns you have accumulated in those areas, and be willing to discard any that are unskillful. Many people hope that one day someone will come along, or something will suddenly happen, like a flash of lightning, and transform their life completely. You can waste your whole life looking for happiness to arrive from the outside. A quiet, basic contentment is our birthright; it is already inside us. Mindfulness gives us a vehicle that can drive us straight to the place where it lives.

FINAL WORDS: Truc transformation is difficult. It begins with small changes, changes in how we breathe, eat, walk, and drive.

24

Look Deeply into Food

THE EXERCISE: When you eat, take a moment to look into the food or drink as if you could see backward, into its history. Use the power of imagination to see where it comes from and how many people might have been involved in bringing it to your plate. Think of the people who planted, weeded, and harvested the food, the truckers who transported it, the food packagers and plant workers, the grocers and check-out people, and the family members or other cooks who prepared the food. Thank those people before you take a sip or a bite.

Reminding Yourself

Post signs reading "Look into Your Food" in locations where you usually eat, such as in the kitchen or on the dining room table.

Discoveries

At the monastery we say a chant before meals that contains this line: "We reflect on the effort that brought us this food and consider how it comes to us." As with anything that you repeat several times a day, chanting these words does not mean that at each meal we actually think about all the people involved in bringing our food to our bowls. We might be vaguely aware of the cook in the kitchen and grateful to him or her if the meal is tasty. Hence this practice.

We have the advantage of growing much of our food at our monastery. Working in the garden and greenhouses opens our mind to how much work goes into bringing the lettuce and carrots to our salad. We are grateful to our neighbor as we shovel manure from his barn into our truck, shovel it back out of the truck, and layer it onto our compost pile along with scraps from the kitchen and clippings from the mower. Anyone who has helped with our annual canning gains a new respect for applesauce after picking many barrelsful of apples from neighbors' trees, then washing, cutting, cooking, pureeing, and canning hundreds of quarts of fruit. Even though we are closer than most modern people to the labor involved in being able to sit down at a table of food and eat, when we do this deep-looking practice, we find that we still take many foods for granted, particularly those in packages, such as flour, sugar, salt, cheese, oats, and milk.

We do this exercise frequently, as part of our mindful-eating practice. It helps us look with the inner eye in order to see the scores of people whose life energy contributed to the food on our plates: the cook, the checkout clerk, the shelf stockers, the delivery drivers, the people in the packaging plants, the farmers, and the migrant workers.

When my husband and I had young children, we spent a few minutes in silence before meals contemplating who brought us our food. We were living in a big city, where most children thought that all food, including the fresh produce, came from the supermarket, mysteriously manufactured there behind the scenes, possibly from plastic. Even many intelligent adults do not know where food comes from. When a guest cooking soup at the monastery asked for onions, I went outside and returned with two I had pulled from the garden. He was appalled. What were those strange things with dirt on them?

Once the BBC did an April Fools' Day spoof on TV, a lovely news short on the abundant spaghetti harvest in Switzerland. (You can view it by searching online for "spaghetti harvest Switzerland BBC.") The film showed costumed women gaily picking long strands of pasta from trees and happy patrons being served "fresh-picked spaghetti" in restaurants. Many people contacted the BBC to ask where they could buy a spaghetti tree for their own garden!

Deeper Lessons

When we look deeply into our food, we become aware of our complete dependence on the life energy of countless beings. If you pause to contemplate a single raisin in your cereal bowl and count the number of people who were involved in bringing it to you, going back to the people who planted, pruned, and weeded the grapevine it grew on, it is at least dozens. If you go back much farther, to the origin of cultivated grapes in the Mediterranean, it is tens of thousands. If you add in the nonhuman beings—earthworms, soil bacteria, fungi, bees—it becomes millions of living beings whose life energy flows toward you, manifesting as the raisin in your bowl and ultimately as the life of your cells.

To experience this is to understand deep within your soul the true meaning of communion. Each time we eat or drink, we are coming into union with countless beings. Life dies, enters our body, and becomes life again. This happens over and over until we die, when we give all that energy back. Our body disperses and arises again as many new forms of life.

How can we repay that many beings? Not with money. If we paid each person who handled this raisin a dollar, raisins would be the food only of kings. Can we at least honor them with our grateful awareness, with a mindful moment's appreciation of their hard work before we begin eating?

The Zen teacher Thich Nhat Hanh says,

> A person who practices mindfulness can see things in a tangerine that others are unable to see. An aware person can see the tangerine tree, the tangerine blossoms in the spring, the sunlight and rain which nourished the tangerine. Looking deeply one can see the ten thousand things which have made the tangerine possible . . . and how all these things interact with each other.

FINAL WORDS: The life energy of many beings flows into us as we eat. How best to repay them? By being fully present as we eat.

25

Smile

THE EXERCISE: For one week, please allow yourself to smile. Notice the expression on your face. Notice it from the inside—lips turned up or down? Teeth clenched? Tension and frown lines between the eyebrows? When you pass a mirror or reflective window, sneak a look at your expression. When you notice a neutral or negative expression, smile. This does not have to be a wide smile; it can be a small smile, like the smile of the Mona Lisa.

Reminding Yourself

Post the word *smile* or a picture of smiling lips in various places, including on mirrors, and perhaps on your computer, on the dashboard of your car, on the back of the front door, and on your phone. You can try smiling when you talk on the phone, at stop lights, or whenever your computer shows the "wait" icon. When you meditate, try a soft "inner smile" like the smile on the face of the Buddha.

Discoveries

Some people feel resistant to doing this exercise. They feel that it is "fake" or unnatural to smile all the time. If they check a mirror several times a day, however, they may be quite surprised to find that all the time they were assuming that their face held a pleasant look, their habitual expression was actually negative—a slight frown, a downturn to the corners of the mouth that looks disapproving. Once people realize this, they often undertake to adjust their face to look more positive.

At the monastery we once tried a more extreme version of smiling practice called "laughing yoga." No matter how we felt, at nine a.m. we all gathered in a circle, rang a bell, and laughed for two full minutes. Laughter that at first seemed fake became genuine as we watched one another laugh. People found that once they overcame their resistance to smiling or laughing even when they didn't feel like it, these practices were quite enjoyable and induced a positive mood. Once a teacher assigned a somewhat morose student the practice of "grinning like an idiot" for an entire weeklong retreat. The man, a veteran of many long retreats, said it was the most relaxed, enjoyable one he'd ever done.

There is a lot of interesting research on smiling. In all human cultures, smiles express happiness. Smiling is innate, not learned. Every baby starts to smile around four months, even if they have been blind from birth. Babies show different smiles when they see their mothers ("genuine") and when approached by strangers ("social" smiles that involve the mouth but not the eyes). Smiles are powerful social signals. People shown pictures of different ethnic groups are more positively inclined toward any group shown smiling. Smiles help defuse anger in others; they can be distinguished from negative facial expressions at a hundred meters—the distance of a spear throw.

Research shows that smiling has many beneficial physiological effects. It lowers blood pressure, enhances the immune system, and releases natural painkillers (endorphins) and a natural antidepressant (serotonin). People who smile in a wholehearted way live, on average, seven years longer than those who do not have a habit of smiling. Smiling also makes people more likely to see you as more attractive, more successful, younger, and as someone they like.

Deeper Lessons

Smiles are contagious. Often people who emerge from retreats are puzzled to find other people smiling at them, even strangers they encounter on the street or in a grocery store. Then they realize that their inner relaxed state has emerged as an outer smile and that others are simply responding to that smile. The benefit is returned: when people smile back at us, our mood improves.

When we smile, it doesn't just affect the moods of others, it also affects our own emotions. There is feedback from the facial muscles to the brain. The Zen teacher Thich Nhat Hanh says, "Sometimes your joy is the source of your smile, but sometimes your smile can be the source of your joy."

When you smile, and even when you simply stretch your mouth as if you were smiling, your emotions take an upturn. In fact, when people use Botox to erase facial wrinkles, their ability to move the facial muscles involved in smiling decreases, and so does the strength of their emotions, positive and negative. Research on smiling clearly shows that controlling the face can help control the mind and the emotions it produces. Dale Jorgensen, an expert on the effects of smiling, says,

> I've thought about this quite a bit. What I've found has reinforced one of my guiding principles, that we really are in charge of our destinies. We do have influence over what happens to us by virtue of our actions. Smiling is a case in which a simple act can have profound effects on the kinds of experiences we have with other people and how they treat us.

The Buddha is always depicted with a gentle smile on his face. It is an inspiring smile, a smile born of the joy of mindful awareness, of a person who is content in all circumstances, even at his death.

FINAL WORDS: If smiling has such clear positive effects on us and those around us, perhaps we should take up a "serious" lifelong smiling practice.

Beginning a Sitting Meditation Practice

Someone once asked me, "Do we need to learn to meditate? Isn't mindfulness enough?" It depends. Enough for what? Is mindfulness enough to make you happier? Yes. It is enough to dispel the common ennui, pervasive anxiety, subtle depression, and restlessness that often beset us. Medical studies show that mindfulness practice can relieve pain and many ailments of body and mind, from asthma to psoriasis, from eating disorders to depression. That simply being present, inhabiting our lives more fully, can make us happier and healthier is a truly wonderful discovery.

Mindfulness practices are a kind of meditation-in-action, or prayer-in-action. There is another aspect of mindfulness that involves sitting still. We often call it sitting practice. When the body is still, the mind can also become quieter. When the mind settles, we are able to get some space around the tangle of our thoughts. We have a chance to look deeply into the important questions of our life.

When the individual mind, with all its memories and worries, is still, we have access to a deep stream of wisdom that can emerge as insights, powerful enough to change the course of our life. That emergence is called by various names: openings, awakening to Truth, the voice of the divine.

No matter what it is called, when we

are able to experience it within ourselves, our life is transformed. We are no longer afraid to live in this unpredictable, complex world. We know that we, like all beings, belong in this world, exactly where we are and exactly as we are.

Here are basic sitting meditation instructions. I encourage you to find a teacher who can guide you further.

Basic Meditation Instructions

Sit down on a chair or on a cushion on the floor. Sit in a way that feels relaxed but upright, allowing plenty of room in your chest and abdomen for breathing. (If you are unable to sit up, you can meditate lying down.)

Focus your attention on your breath. Find the places in your body where you are most aware of the sensations of breathing. Don't try to alter your breath—your body knows very well how to breathe—just turn your attention to the breath.

Rest your attention in the constantly changing sensations of breathing for the full duration of the in-breath and the full duration of the out-breath. Each time your mind wanders away from awareness of the breath (which it is likely to do often), gently bring it back.

This is the experience of being relaxed but fully present, as if we had awakened on a vacation day, with nothing special to do except to take simple pleasure in just sitting and breathing.

Continue for up to twenty or thirty minutes, a good amount of time for one meditation session. It is also fine to go longer. It is best to meditate every day, making this part of your personal health care, like taking a shower (for your mind). On a very busy day you may have to cut the time. Five or ten minutes each day is better than two hours once a month. I find that each minute of meditation is returned twofold or more in clarity, equanimity, and efficiency during a busy day.

Further Ways to Practice

Some of the exercises in this book can be extended into periods of meditation, contemplation, or prayer. Be creative. Here are a few examples:

Chapter 3: Appreciate Your Hands

As you meditate, open your awareness to the feelings within your hands, particularly where they touch each other. Christians may wish to meditate upon "These are the hands of God."

Chapter 10: Just Three Breaths

During meditation, for three breaths, keep your mind completely open and receptive, free of thoughts. Then relax and let your mind wander as it will. In a few minutes, once again, let all thoughts drop, and pay full attention to the subject of prayer or meditation for just three breaths. Repeat.

Chapter 21: Listen like a Sponge

During meditation or contemplation, listen very carefully to all the sounds you hear, both obvious and subtle. Listen as if at any minute you might hear an important message.

Suggested Reading

The following are a few of the most clearly written and popular books on mindfulness:

Gunaratana, Bhante Henepola. *Mindfulness in Plain English*. Boston: Wisdom Publications, 1991.

Hanh, Thich Nhat. *The Miracle of Mindfulness: An Introduction to the Practice of Meditation*. Boston: Beacon Press, 1999.

Hanh, Thich Nhat. *Happiness: Essential Mindfulness Practices*. Berkeley: Parallax Press, 2009.

Kabat-Zinn, Jon. *Full Catastrophe Living: Using the Wisdom of Your Body and Mind to Face Stress, Pain, and Illness*. New York: Delacorte Press, 1990.

Kabat-Zinn, Jon. *Wherever You Go, There You Are: Mindfulness Meditation in Everyday Life*. New York: Hyperion, 1994.

You may also be interested in reading my previous book, *Mindful Eating: A Guide to Rediscovering a Healthy and Joyful Relationship with Food* (Boston: Shambhala Publications, 2009).

Acknowledgments

I am grateful to my teachers, the Zen masters Maezumi Roshi and Shodo Harada Roshi. I have learned much about mindfulness by watching them do ordinary tasks such as opening envelopes or making tea. I am grateful to all the people who have undertaken these mindfulness exercises so earnestly over the past twenty years and who passed their discoveries and insights on to me. I am also grateful to Eden Steinberg, whose unfailing editorial eye helped create a better book than I could write alone.

About the Author

Jan Chozen Bays, MD, is a pediatrician, a meditation teacher, the author of *Mindful Eating*, and the abbess of Great Vow Zen Monastery in Oregon, where the mindfulness exercises in this book were developed and refined. She is also a wife, mother, and grandmother. She likes to garden, work in clay, and play the marimba. For more information visit www.greatvow.org/teachers.htm.

Library of Congress
Cataloging-in-Publication Data

Bays, Jan Chozen, author.
[How to train a wild elephant and other adventures in mindfulness]
Mindfulness on the go: simple meditation practices you can do anywhere /
Jan Chozen Bays.
pages cm—(Shambhala pocket classics)
ISBN 978-1-61180-170-5 (paperback)
1. Spiritual life—Buddhism.
2. Meditation—Buddhism. I. Title.
BQ5670.B39 2014
294.3'4435—dc23
2014005488

Shambhala Pocket Classics

THE ART OF PEACE
Teachings of the Founder of Aikido
by Morihei Ueshiba
Compiled and translated
by John Stevens

THE ART OF WAR
by Sun Tzu
Translated by Thomas Cleary

AWAKENING LOVING-KINDNESS
by Pema Chödrön

DHAMMAPADA
The Sayings of the Buddha
Rendered by Thomas Byrom

HAGAKURE
The Book of the Samurai
by Yamamoto Tsunetomo
Translated by William Scott Wilson

I CHING
The Book of Change
Translated by Thomas Cleary

THE MAN WHO PLANTED TREES
by Jean Giono

THE POCKET
CHÖGYAM TRUNGPA
Compiled and edited by
Carolyn Gimian

THE POCKET DALAI LAMA
Edited by Mary Craig

THE POCKET EMILY DICKINSON
Edited by Brenda Hillman

THE POCKET HAIKU
Compiled and translated by Sam Hamill

THE POCKET KEN WILBER
Edited by Colin Bigelow

THE POCKET PEMA CHÖDRÖN
Edited by Eden Steinberg

THE POCKET RUMI
Edited by Kabir Helminski

THE POCKET SAMURAI
Translated and edited by
William Scott Wilson

THE POCKET THICH NHAT HANH
Compiled and edited by
Melvin McLeod

THE POCKET THOMAS MERTON
Edited by Robert Inchausti

THE POCKET
TIBETAN BUDDHISM READER
Edited by Reginald A. Ray

THE POCKET ZEN READER
Edited by Thomas Cleary

PRACTICING PEACE
by Pema Chodron

SHAMBHALA
The Sacred Path of the Warrior
by Chögyam Trungpa

TAO TEH CHING
by Lao Tzu
Translated by John C. H. Wu

TEACHINGS OF THE BUDDHA
Edited by Jack Kornfield